The Gifted and Talented in Art
A Guide to Program Planning

An imaginative landscape based upon personal recollection. Students should be encouraged to try both real and fanciful approaches to still lifes, portraits, landscapes and other aspects of their environment.

The Gifted and Talented in Art
A Guide to Program Planning

Al Hurwitz

Head, Department of Art Teacher Education
The Maryland Institute, College of Art

Davis Publications, Inc.
Worcester, Massachusetts

To Aunt Lena and Uncle I., for a lifetime of affection and support.

PRINTED IN THE UNITED STATES OF AMERICA

Library of Congress Catalog Card Number: 82-74002

ISBN: 0-87192-143-X

DESIGNER   Penny Darras-Maxwell

COVER illustration is an abstract landscape by a twelve-year-old Canadian
boy.

10   9   8   7   6   5   4   3   2   1

Contents

Introduction   6

Part One   Defining Artistic Giftedness   11
 1   Where Does Talent Begin?   13
 2   Artistic Giftedness and Modes of Intelligence   15
 3   Characteristics of the Visually Gifted   18
 4   Critical Sensitivity: The Unexplored Dimension   28

Part Two   Planning a Program   31
 5   Initiators: Who Gets Things Going?   32
 6   Funding: Who Pays?   34
 7   Identification: Who Will Be Served?   42
 8   Curriculum: What Shall Be Taught?   61
 9   Location: Where Shall We Meet?   81
 10   Evaluation: How Far Have We Come?   83
 11   Dissemination: Letting People Know   93

Part Three   Model Programs   95
 12   Examples of Programs   96

Appendix I   Sample Forms   122

Appendix II   Organizations for the Gifted   138

Bibliography   139

Index   142

Acknowledgements   144

Introduction

This book provides basic information on creating supportive, stimulating environments for children and adolescents gifted in the visual arts. Guidelines for developing, funding, implementing and evaluating art programs are provided. Model programs and guidelines for identifying the students to be served by them are also described.

The nature of visual giftedness is often misunderstood. Artistic talent often reflects abilities other than skillful, accurate rendering and the effective use of art media. Although these are certainly commonly observed characteristics, talent can also draw upon intellect, creativity, and personal attitudes and traits which, if neglected, can keep a child from realizing his or her artistic potential.

A classic example of the multifaceted nature of talent is Leonardo da Vinci. His inquiring mind and consuming curiosity about all aspects of life made him a master artist and a problem solver in such diverse fields as architecture, city planning, and military strategy. Some Renaissance figures of today, although admittedly of a lesser order, are art directors and industrial designers. They usually begin as visual artists, but end up as business experts and social analysts, fields not normally associated with art.

Any art program, therefore, that purports to serve the visually gifted should be planned to extend all the talents the children bring to the program. Students who draw well must be challenged to use this skill in new contexts; those who stand out for their advanced modeling ability must be shown how other untried materials can extend the sculptural impulse. In the section on curriculum in Part II specific activities are listed that require students to call upon related modes of intelligence.

A Glance Backward

Attention to students with high ability in art is not new, although efforts on behalf of such students have greatly accelerated in the past decade. In the early thirties New York's Board of Education ran a program for artistically gifted students in conjunction with New York University. The Maryland Institute of Art has offered Saturday morning classes since the mid-twenties. In the early forties, the education department of the Cleveland Museum of Art, under the guidance of Thomas Munro and Betty Lark-Horowitz, conducted research into the nature of artistically talented children.

The New York program was based largely upon teacher referrals, while other institutions relied on an open door policy under the assumption that high interest in art would separate high achievers from their classmates. Contemporary programs may employ multiple techniques for selection and are far more aggressive in seeking out minority children from lower economic levels. Today's selection methods reflect a more sophisticated view of artistic talent and recognize that visual ability is often related to other modes of intelligence. This is quite different from the pre-World War II selection process in which an art teacher informally contacted a museum or an art center about a talented student.

In the past decade, federal monies for gifted students in all areas has risen from two to ten million dollars a year. The amount allocated to innovative arts programming will continue to rest upon the ingenuity and aggressiveness of teachers and administrators in conceiving and preparing the right proposals. This book is an aid to putting together such proposals.

Serving the Gifted: The Controversial Side

Art educators have always been sensitive to those who question the place of general art courses in the schools on the misguided premise that these courses exclusively serve artistically talented students and therefore have no place in tax-supported institutions that are intended to serve all of the children. If the case for art education must be made for the values it holds for all students — bright or slow, poor or rich — how can one justify any program that deals with no more than five percent of the school enrollment?

In the past decade, however, the idea of serving minorities with special problems became not only accepted but mandated. Once the American public accepted the concept of special needs in such areas as mental retardation, emotional disorders, and physical disabilities, it was inevitable that another group of children would have to be dealt with: those who were capable of exceptional levels of achievement, but were not working up to full potential. This was the last group to be included in this concept and included artistically talented students who were high achievers or who were not working at optimum level.

The arguments against and in favor of singling out gifted students in all areas are numerous. The following arguments have been directed at programs of recognition for both artistic and academically talented children.

Arguments against Special Attention for the Gifted

- The most capable will always take care of themselves and rise to the top. Since the "problem" children are already getting so much attention, the schools should concentrate on students of average ability.
- Special programs harden society's class lines because achievement is so often related to socio-economic environment. This, in turn, breeds charges of elitism, a trait associated with private rather than with public schools. The separation of the gifted from their classmates thus may have racial overtones since the children of the poor are less likely to show success.
- Special programs for the gifted draw lines between children that can be socially damaging since they divide children into groups of "winners" and "losers."
- Such programs do not deal with those whose gifts may emerge at a later date, for the so-called late bloomers.
- Programs for the gifted instill attitudes of competitiveness among students, parents, and even schools. While this may be acceptable in athletics, it has no place in creative areas especially on the elementary level.
- Singling out children for any reason may render them a disservice since they may come to see themselves as "better" than their classmates.

Arguments in Favor of Focusing Attention on the Gifted

- Most public education is inadequate because instruction has always been geared to the middle group. Gifted students have as much right to special consideration as children who are handicapped.
- The charge of elitism is questionable since giftedness resides in all cultural groups, as demonstrated by many of the illustrations in this book. Many programs have been created with poor, minority children in mind. Recognition of high ability in any area may be a key factor in sustaining positive self-images of children from disadvantaged backgrounds.

Talent is evidenced at an early age, usually through drawing. This four-year-old's work already shows the complexity and story-telling power of the gifted child.

- Programs for the gifted can upgrade and improve other programs; they often have a spill-over effect on general classes.
- While no single program can accommodate gifted children of all ages, several offerings based upon levels of maturity can serve those who display talent at an early age and those whose abilities may not emerge until adolescence.
- Special programs create a learning climate wherein gifted children do not feel peculiar and can give full rein to their abilities. Working with peers (classmates of equal ability) provides greater challenge because children learn from each other as well as from teachers.
- When a talented student no longer stands out as "class artist" or resident genius, he or she will tend to be less self-centered and have a more realistic view of his or her abilities. This principle works best in any situation where students work with their peers. Students often discover this in the first year of art school. ("If I am no longer the best, what exactly am I?")

In answering the charge of elitism, it could be pointed out that schools have too often been remiss in seeking out gifted, disadvantaged children. We cannot assume that talent is automatically recognized and supported by authorities or that it is sufficiently self-nurtured by the students. The policy of affirmative action calls for more than equal job opportunities: it implies equal standards of education in all areas for all children. In this regard a sound program for the gifted is one safeguard against the charge of elitism.

Having reviewed the pros and cons, it should be made clear that there has never been an instance of an art teacher abandoning a general art program for one that serves some elite minority. Decisions about programs are made by school committees, which, in turn, reflect the pressures of the taxpayers who voted them into office. We need a broadly based art education: the across-the-board classes that serve children within the framework of general education, and programs that recognize that general classes may not adequately satisfy the needs of the few who will ultimately comprise the aesthetic leadership of our country. The painters, designers, craftsmen and craftswomen, architects, and museum directors of the future are in our classes at this very moment. If history can tell us anything, it is that these students need the same kind of support given our future scientists, doctors, and engineers.

Defining Artistic Giftedness

Part One

This preschooler shows an early
— and big — interest in art.

1 Where Does Talent Begin?

An artist is often someone who, at an early age, felt uncommon satisfaction with visual expression of one kind or another. A satisfactory explanation has yet to be given for the inner psychic source that sets this impulse on its way, but it probably has a lot to do with the pleasure principle.

Howard Gardner puts it this way: "For it is in the activity of the young child, his preconscious sense of form, his willingness to explore and to solve problems that arise, his capacity to take risks, his affective needs, which must be worked out in a symbolic realm — that we find the crucial seeds of the greatest artistic achievement."[1]

The source of the artistic impulse is not as important as the fact that somehow it does surface, often before school age. Its nourishment may therefore lie more in the hands of the parents than in those of the school teachers. Since a large percentage of people in art-related fields come from homes in which art is an important part of life, one cannot dismiss the effect of environment.

Parents need not be professionals to play a critical role in nourishing the talent of their preschool children. Even if they lack experience or knowledge of art, parents can always:

- Have drawing supplies on hand. (Soft pencils, fine-line, felt-tipped pens, crayons, and paper in a variety of sizes.
- Designate a special display area for their children's art. (The refrigerator door will do if there is no other space.)
- Discuss a child's drawings with him or her.
- Set an example by making an occasional effort to draw themselves.

It all amounts to taking this part of the child's life seriously.

Artistically gifted children often do as well academically as intellectually superior students. All applicants to art schools and universities meet the same academic admission standards. One can, therefore, propose the idea that our artistic, intellectual, and creative potentials are rooted in a common pool of distinct, yet related abilities, which at a later date unite as they are called upon to serve a personal or vocational end. The visual side that we see, while emerging initially through drawing, may take other forms of expression as the child is drawn to the sensuousness of color, or the spatial/tactile na-

A collection of Christmas drawings by a six-year-old girl, Masami Onada. As a Japanese girl living in the United States, Masami incorporated many Western holiday motifs into her work. The quality of her line, her handling of space and proportion, and the sheer prodigality of her output mark her as one of the most gifted children the author has encountered.

ture of sculpture, or the imagery of time and motion that only movie-making can provide.

Books that deal with children's art place a disproportionate emphasis upon drawing, a tendency that can give a limited, not to say inaccurate, picture of where visual giftedness resides. Children will never realize they are potential photographers unless someone gives them access to cameras. Therefore, one major function of the schools is to expand the repertoire of experience by providing materials and equipment not available elsewhere. By failing to do this, schools can present a severely limited view of the possibilities of visual expression. However, whatever other art forms we may pursue, we usually begin by drawing. Call it graphic investigation or symbolization, artists begin by making marks on paper, on walls, with pencil, crayons, pen, or brush.

[1]Howard Gardner, *Artful Scribbles: The Significance of Children's Drawings* (New York: Basic Books, 1980)

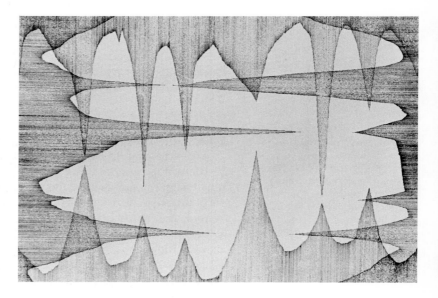

2 Artistic Giftedness and Modes of Intelligence

It is the writer's view that high visual ability rests largely on intensity and commitment. Whatever most children are capable of accomplishing, the gifted surpass in quality, love of work, and amount of time spent. The spiral that moves from average ability, to aptitude and flair, to giftedness and talent, and on to the level of prodigy and genius is a matter of the acceleration of what one writer has described as the "capacity for imaginative creation, original thought, invention or discovery."[1]

A U.S. Department of Education publication[2] offers the following official designation of giftedness and talent, which is often referred to by proposal writers:

> Gifted and talented children are those identified by professionally qualified persons who, by virtue of outstanding abilities, are capable of high performance. These are children who require differentiated educational programs in order to realize their contribution to self and society. Children capable of high performance include those with demonstrated achievement and/or potential ability in any of the following areas, singly or in combination:
>
> 1. General intellectual ability
> 2. Specific academic aptitude
> 3. Creative or productive thinking
> 4. Leadership ability
> 5. Visual and performing arts
> 6. Psychomotor ability

As states and local school districts initiated programs for the gifted and talented, they accepted the USOE definition or chose to amend it. New York State, as an example, decided to delete points 3 and 6, adding in their place "Ethical Sensitivity" and "Moral Responsibility" (1981). Definitions, however thoughtfully construed, are rarely found acceptable to all concerned. Even the seemingly reasonable USOE's definitions can be questioned on several points.

"High performance," of course, is not easily defined, and adults unfamiliar with art will often confuse it with flair or aptitude, which can be defined as a degree above average yet lacking in that qualitative dimension that puts other students in the realm of talent. "Qualified authority" is another term which lacks a clear definition. Being an artist may not be enough to make someone a qualified authority. The people who select the "qualified authority" must themselves possess exceptional qualifications. Working from the principle that "it takes one to know one," art specialists (teachers or supervisors) should be consulted when deciding upon the credentials of those who must pass judgment on visual giftedness.

The USDE definition, while sufficiently broad to include artistic talent, does pose some provocative questions regarding the relationships that exist among abilities. For one thing, the traits listed in this definition are difficult to separate. Creative thinking is a process that artists, performers, and scientists all share. Leadership ability also overlaps in many areas. For example, in the case of theatrical or art directors, it is virtually impossible for these traits to function without general intellectual ability; nor can a potter function without psychomotor ability, regardless of the uniqueness of his vision. The USDE definition also does not take into account crucial motivational characteristics such as tenacity and persistence.

Despite the wide range of talents mentioned above, a review of admissions criteria for academic programs for the gifted reveals that intellectual ability is still the major requirement. This standard often applies to art programs as well.

Three Related Modes of Intelligence

Before the recognition of high ability accelerated during the last decade, giftedness was judged by how well a student did on the I.Q. test, which tested a student's facility with such things as word usage, analogies, abstractions, and classifications. Psychologists, however, eventually discovered that other dimensions of the intellect needed to be recognized and encouraged. Interest then developed in another aspect of intelligence: creativity.

Art teachers, of course, have been using the term *creativity* for decades, but in a vague, romantic, ill-defined way. Today's tests on creativity present problems that require divergent thinking, problem-solving ability, fluency, flexibility, originality, and elaboration. Instead of asking for correct answers, these tests may ask children to improve products, suggest unusual uses for commonplace objects, and speculate about the relations between cause and effect. They also break away from purely verbal/written responses and may ask for picture-making. Psychologists discovered that such modes of

An example of obsessive concern with a single problem: a rambling, 30-inch sculpture composed of toothpicks. The student later went on to work in other three-dimensional media.

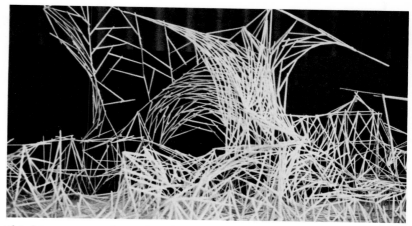

thinking were universal ones, shared by all highly creative people, and not limited to artists.

Joseph Renzulli calls our attention to another facet of intelligence: task commitment. He describes this as "the ability to involve oneself totally in a problem or area for an extended period of time."[3] Task commitment can border on the obsessive and parents and teachers may be dismayed by the kind of total absorption that often leads a child to ignore other obligations, such as household tasks and academic responsibilities. It should be noted that parents rarely complain about high academic achievers not paying enough attention to the arts. Indeed, the child with a particularly rough road to travel is the one who feels deeply about both areas and feels that a choice must be made between the two.

We are now confronted by three aspects of intelligence, all of which have implications for the visually gifted child: intellectual, creative, and attitudinal. The ways in which these aptitudes are incorporated into special art programs and used at later stages of development may well determine the kind of art career a child may elect to pursue.

Talent in art is probably just the tip of an iceberg of abilities. It is a source of intense satisfaction embedded in a cluster of aptitudes that emerge and realign themselves within the context of a particular profession. Since we are in an age when new careers are constantly created and ever-new connections are made between existing professions, special programs for the artistically gifted should alert students to what lies beyond high performance in the area of immediate interest.

[1]Howard Gardner, *Artful Scribbles: The Significance of Children's Drawings* (New York: Basic Books, 1980)

[2]U.S. Department of Education, *Education of the Gifted and Talented: Report to Congress* (Washington, D.C.: Government Printing Office, 1972)

[3]Joseph Renzulli, "What Makes Giftedness: A Redefinition," *Phi Delta Kappan* 60, no. 3 (November 1978)

3 Characteristics of the Visually Gifted

Two sets of characteristics are associated with children talented in art: behavioral traits and characteristics of their artwork. It is not always easy to separate these characteristics since personal behavior so often determines the nature of the art product. No child, however talented, can reflect all of the characteristics that follow. It is unlikely, however, that one who lacks all or most of them possesses special talent in art.

Behavioral Characteristics

Early Evidence

Children who are gifted in art usually begin young, in many cases before school and often as early as age three. This has been borne out in interviews with students, artists, and artists' parents. One study of students of the Art Institute of Chicago showed that more than twenty-five percent of those interviewed had very clear memories of interest in art before the age of ten.[1]

Emergence through Drawing

Study the case histories of artists and you will find that drawing predominates. Giftedness first evidences itself through the pencil or crayon, and for the most part, will remain in this realm of expression until the child is either motivated to try other forms of expression or until drawing becomes boring. Drawing dominates not only because of the accessibiity of the media, but because it can convey detailed information about a subject, a much more difficult task to perform with a paint brush. Given a brush in the primary grades, children usually will begin by using it as an extension of the drawing impulse and will use it to outline shapes and then to fill in between the lines.

Rapidity of Development

Every art teacher is familiar with the pattern of children's progression through certain stages of visual development.[1] They begin by scribbling, then the scribbles are named, differentiated, and combined for various purposes. Objects float freely and then are related, and predictable symbols appear from the children's environment: sky, sun, birds, houses, trees. This process continues until around the ages of nine to eleven years when a period of frustration sets in as the child measures his own efforts against the real world and images from mass media, which to the child are no less real. The gifted child often traverses such stages at an accelerated pace and can often condense normal progress to short periods.

This ten-year-old girl is well beyond the level of spatial awareness for her age in this fantasy of figures flying over flowers. Her compositional control and drawing ability place her in the secondary level.

The sense of gesture, proportion, and ease of connection among parts of the body are in advance of this thirteen-year-old's classmates.

Although gifted children may progress through stages of symbolization at a more rapid pace than others, the field of art has yet to produce a child prodigy on the level of musical sophistication shown by the young Mozart. One very interesting exception may be an autistic English child named Nadia who at the age of three-and-a-half began to draw with the skill of a gifted child five times her age. Her use of such advanced techniques as foreshortening and contour line drawing plus her own loose, personal handling of line were remarkable manifestations of giftedness that lay close to genius. It is interesting to note that as Nadia improved through therapy, her skill as an artist declined.

Extended Concentration

Visually gifted children stay with an artistic problem longer than do other students. In part this is because they derive greater pleasure from their work. They also see more possibilities in the task they have selected or been assigned. They are not as apt to socialize as their peers and often prefer to work alone rather than in a group. Any teacher, therefore, who provides only large tables for groups of four or more can set up stumbling blocks for those children who need to be alone with their thoughts. This is particularly true for the art room in the junior high school, which too often lacks diversity of seating possibilities.

Self-directedness

For artistically gifted children, school is not the only place to pursue their interests. They are highly self-motivated and have the drive to work on their own. Not only may they draw or paint while others are watching television, they often prefer art activity to television, sports, or other forms of entertainment.

Possible Inconsistency with Creative Behavior

It is a mistake to assume that the behavior of the artistically gifted is consistent with characteristics that we associate with creativity in general. Often the exact opposite is true. For example, risk taking is frequently cited as a hallmark of the creative person. We like to think of an accomplished painter or dancer as someone who does not flinch from the prospect of failure in new situations. Because gifted students have invested a great deal of themselves in developing mastery in a certain idiom, they are unwilling or unable to experiment in new areas.

Nadia, an autistic British child, astounded the world with her realistic drawings of horses, produced between the ages of three-and-a-half and seven. As her ability to speak increased, her graphic "gift" diminished, raising questions about the relationship of graphic development to other mental growth.

24

This drawing is very detailed. Note the bridle, tunic, trumpet and hand, together with the inappropriate and disturbing face, and squirrel on the horse's side. Drawn at approximately 5 years 6 months.

This study of a city hall by a twelfth-grade student combines photography, watercolor, and low-relief cardboard sculpture in a unique multimedia work. It is an example of self-directed personal discovery through experimentation with materials and processes.

Success won through long hours of practice is not easily relinquished in favor of journeys into the unknown. This is where a sensitive teacher can make all the difference. The reluctance of young people to lose face before their peers tends to bring out attitudes of extreme conservatism when confronting the new. One of the best arguments for formal schooling is the opportunity it can provide for overcoming such attitudes.

Art As Escape   When presented with a subject a visually gifted student feels is difficult or nongratifying, art may become a retreat from responsibility and an excessive amount of time may be spent drawing or working in other media. Such behavior often is accompanied by the kind of fantasizing reflected in the artwork and poses a difficult problem for the teacher who must decide to (a) support this tendency and guide it toward more constructive channels, or (b) seek ways of making the stumbling block more attractive, challenging. No talent, however impressive, is beneficial if used as an escape from other responsibilities, and precocity should not relieve a child from demands required of his peers. An excess of any behavior bears watching.

Fluency of Idea and Expression   Visual and conceptual fluency, observable from middle elementary age on, is perhaps the most significant characteristic of all since it lies closest to the behavior of the trained artist. Visually fluent children may have more ideas than they have time to depict. Asked to draw a still life, they will include details missed by others; given a story to illustrate, they will draw multiple rather than single episodes. Their memory banks hold more and what is not recalled can be invented. If a mural is in the making and suggestions are solicited, visually fluent children will have more ideas than can be accommodated. Give each child in the class a sketchbook, and those of the fluent children will be the first filled. They draw the way most people talk, because through drawing they maintain a dialogue with the world. Through this ability they visualize events and forms that have not previously existed.

Calculating Capacity   Gifted children from upper elementary school age on also have what Howard Gardner in *Artful Scribbles* terms "calculating capacity," that is, a superior ability to utilize past information in new contexts. For

Two masterful approaches to watercolor technique by senior high school students: the landscape is controlled and carefully drawn; the animal portrait is loose, free flowing, and powerful in its impact.

example, having mastered the figure in movement from a few basic positions taken from copying or from life drawing, visually gifted students can use this information to render figures in new situations.

Characteristics of the Artwork

Behavior is certainly not the only means of identifying visually gifted students. Their artwork is an obvious give-away and shows certain characteristics seldom noted in the work of other children.

The writer has dealt with literally thousands of examples of child and adolescent art; judged hundreds of portfolios for the Interational Baccalaureate Secondary Diploma, Advanced Placement, and ARTS (Arts Recognition Talent Search); been a close observer of the National Scholastic Award competition; and surveyed the majority of textbooks that deal with student art. The characteristics that follow are based upon personal observation and the observations of other writers. These characteristics will probably not be new to many art teachers, but they may hold a few surprises for parents and classroom teachers. Some of these characteristics may put a few myths to rest. Not all of the traits listed apply to all ages, nor do all talented children possess a full range of these characteristics in equal portion. Indeed, one of the hazards of being gifted is the possibility of developing certain imbalances, not all of them positive.

Verisimilitude Although most children develop the desire to depict people and other subjects from the environment in the upper elementary years, gifted children develop both the skills and the inclination at an earlier age. In the period from ten to fourteen years the urge to get things right emerges in the form of comic strips, illustrations for science fiction, and, more recently, for those areas where science fiction overlaps with mythology and fantasy. Although many students share this interest, only the talented can handle those skills of shading, proportion, perspective, and anatomy that make this form of expression so effective. The narrative, storytelling interests that were begun at a much earlier stage, will, on the secondary level, join forces with the acceleration of technical skill to produce work that can be professional in nature. Comic strips become more artful and interest in the human form is not only sustained but increased. In all cases, visually gifted students seem to grasp more easily the underlying structure of forms. It is not unusual for senior high students to surpass their art teachers in handling the skills needed for realistic portrayal.

Compositional Control

In picture-making, the elements that we associate with composition, color, space, and movement are handled with greater sensitivity by visually gifted students. Color is blended and mixed rather than used directly, the forms within a work are consciously linked rather than randomly placed. Compositional structure is deliberate as well as intuitive, particularly in cases where the student wants to create a particular effect. Composition or visual coherency, is used to make the artistic intention more effective.

Complexity and Elaboration

Gifted children from preschool age on have a sense of complexity that appears as early as the symbolic stages. Most children create schemas that are adequate to their needs. Gifted children elaborate upon their schemas, sometimes as an adjunct of storytelling or fantasizing, sometimes for the sheer fun of adding details of clothes, body parts, or objects related to the schema. Wholes are related to parts as powers of recollection are tested and transformed into a growing repertoire of images. It is in this realm that visualization bears a close relationship to other kinds of development. In the Goodenough-Harris "Draw a Man" test clues to reading readiness are provided by the amount of detail children bring to their drawings. The ability to relate information about objects is intimately connected to intellectual development. Complexity and elaboration are directly related to sensitivity to detail and the use of memory.

Awareness of composition, sensitivity to media, and vivid imagination characterize this airborne structure by a nine-year-old Yugoslavian boy.

This fourth-grader's illustration exudes a sense of compositional authority in the unification of idea and execution. Its sense of style is sustained throughout.

An unusual combination of the use of memory (cars and people) and the handling of real space by a twelve-year-old boy.

Memory and Detail

From their earliest efforts, gifted children are more interested in detail and are more inventive in filling pictorial or three-dimensional space (as in clay modeling). This is partly due to the way they use their memories and partly because their imaginations supply them with more ideas. Good memories, incidentally, are characteristic of all gifted children, but *how* our memories operate is determined by our interests. Musicians, dancers, and actors must all rely upon their memories, yet recollecting sequences of sound, movement, and words are vastly different tasks.

Sensitivity to Art Media

Since one of the characteristics of giftedness is immersion, it follows that one thing that hours of practice will produce is the mastery of any medium that is of particular interest. Where one fourth-grade child may be content to use colors straight out of a box or tube, the gifted child may quickly become bored with packaged colors and combine them to achieve desired effects. Since materials are means to ends, the mastery of media permits a more developed, hence more elegant, product. Such technical control is most pronounced from upper elementary age on.

Because some media are easier to master than others, by the time the artistically gifted student reaches senior high school, pencil technique will be considerably advanced beyond painting, centering on the wheel beyond that of glazing, clay sculpture beyond wood and welding processes, etc. Although the availability of materials can often be a determining factor, a student with a powerful drive to work in a particular material seems to find the resources, be it a better camera, a more versatile brush, or a professional quality acrylic. Art teachers can be a key figure in helping students master a wider range of media, assisting in the search for the materials that students feel they need at a particular time.

Random Improvisation Gifted children often doodle; that is, they improvise with the effects of lines, shapes, and patterns and appear to be conscious of negative areas or spaces between the lines. From upper elementary age on they transfer this absorption with the effects of lines to such subjects as the human face and, like cartoonists, play with minute changes in lines, and note their effects. Art functions as an extended conversation between form and imagination; indeed, the realm of ideas and depiction may be so dominating that technique is often relegated to a position of minor importance. The gifted child thinks through his artwork and creates his own meanings through his ability to invent, depict, and describe.[3]

[1]Gaitskell, Charles D., Hurwitz, Al, and Day, Michael, *Children and Their Art*. (New York: Harcourt, Brace and Jovanovitch, 1982).
[2]Selfe, Lorna, *Nadia: A Case of Extraordinary Drawing Ability in an Autistic Child*. (New York: Harcourt, Brace, and Jovanovitch, 1977).
[3]J. Getzell, "Discovery Oriented Behavior and the Originality of Creative Product: A Study of Artists," *Journal of Personality and Social Psychology*, 1971, Vol.19, pp. 47-52.

Linear improvisation of imaginary faces by a senior high school boy.

4 Critical Sensitivity: The Unexplored Dimension

A distinction must now be made between giftedness in object-making and high sensitivity in critical performance. Some children can verbally relate what they see in ways that go beyond that of their classmates. Their artistic perceptions are sharper, they assimilate art vocabulary more easily, and they can describe what they see or quickly recognize visual phenomena once they are pointed out.

Like all imaginative children, those with perceptive sensitivity love to speculate and to fantasize, but they can be taught to distinguish between these thoughts and responses that require the ability to describe, to analyze, and to interpret. They can make significant connections between the meaning of a work, the intention of the artist, and formal structure (the use of color, line, shape, etc.). They also accept art appreciation as part of art activity because they are interested in the ideas developed through discussion of artwork. Such children can reveal insights into art that are fresh, unexpected, and illuminating.

It is interesting that this aptitude has not been studied as much as high performance with art media. While records exist of case histories of children gifted in drawing or painting, few are available of children's critical-discursive abilities. We would probably be safe in saying that no such discussions ever took place since interest in critical giftedness simply never existed in the schools that today's critics attended as children. In fact, I doubt that anyone thought to ask them their opinions or to teach them how to critically evaluate artwork.

Examine the educational history of art critics, historians, and curators, and you will discover that they come from a variety of disciplines, usually based somewhere on the broad spectrum of the humanities. It is time they came from art education.

Several reasons account for the neglect of art appreciation in our schools. To begin with, there has been a traditional suspicion regarding the role of language, that talking about art is somehow not as legitimate as making it. In addition, teachers in general lack sufficient training in criticism or art history. This is unfortunate because talking about art can effect the making of art and it can provide opportunities for some students to become acquainted with an unexplored side of their intelligence.

For this mixed media study, a nine-year-old Korean child worked directly from nature.

Ralph Smith, editor of the *Journal of Aesthetic Education*, used what he calls the "exemplar approach." In this approach a single work of recognized merit was examined for an extended period of time. In one series of discussions the children in Saturday morning classes were eleven and twelve years old. Discussions never ran less than an hour and at the conclusion of the course, the children requested more sessions. The children were led to the description of artworks and eventually they dealt with problems of interpretation and even analysis. At the conclusion of seven sessions, the class was discussing paintings by Rubens, Piero della Francesco, and Daumier in terms of mood, subject, content, and compositional relationships. One can only imagine the levels such children could attain if such instruction were provided during the course of a year, or during the six years of elementary school. While the number of such students is admittedly small, it is larger than we think. In any case, such children are as deserving of support as are children with other kinds of abilities.

Personal Statement

Several artists and I have used a graduated method of identifying critically gifted children. To begin with, we visit a school not as critics or teachers of art appreciation. Through a previous arrangement with the principal and participating teachers, children are permitted to return to their classrooms at three phases of the presentation without embarrassment or feeling that they are being impolite. I can easily work with two classes, or about fifty children, preferably from upper elementary through the secondary level. In the first phase, I talk about the choice of subject and about the media. I lay out the pallette, sketch in a rough outline of the subject, and lay a tone of color on the drawing after fixing it. This takes about forty minutes and at this stage, the group is told that anyone who wishes to may leave. Not too many will leave since the prospect of seeing color mixed and applied usually holds a powerful attraction. During the complete process, children are invited to ask questions which I answer as I work.

In the second stage, I block in rough masses of color, sometimes working silently, at times thinking aloud about the decisions I make. After a half hour or so of this, I stop to tell them that the second stage is finished and that those who have other things to do may leave. This time a much larger group leaves, since the desire to see pigment in action has been gratified.

In the third phase, I am left with about a quarter of the group. I spend another half hour modifying, adjusting, and placing transitional tones. I now repeat my invitation to ask questions and at the end of this phase, I invite anyone who desires to remain for discussion.

My demonstration is over and now we can get down to some "serious" discussion, about art, about artists, about art making. When the fourth and final phase begins I am left with from five to ten students. I do not know for certain whether they are gifted in the critical or studio areas, but I do know that these children are intensely curious about art and eager to talk about it. If we could repeat this performance in every school in every community and gather all of the fourth phase students, we could help them develop their critical sensibilities — and perhaps ease the way for future art critics, historians, and curators.

Planning a Program

Part Two

5 Initiators: Who Gets Things Going?

Special programs usually begin with an individual imbued with a sense of mission. There are no set rules regarding the nature of initiators. The field is open to anyone with a touch of the entrepreneur. Programs have been founded by art teachers, parents, principals, superintendents, and museum educators.

Some program initiators start from scratch and build a program while others join what already exists. The choices are numerous. A teacher might sponsor a program in a single school, a supervisor might start classes for a district or an entire city, a state department of education might prepare summer programs for students statewide.

Teachers with limited funding can link up with established programs, such as the Advanced Placement Program, the National Scholastic Art Awards, and the Arts Recognition Talent Search (ARTS) (See pages 108 to 110). At a simple level, a teacher could meet periodically with a small group of gifted students to review their work, or a larger group could be invited for special art classes. The model programs in Part III give an idea of the variety of programs that could be instituted.

Before you plunge into the details of starting a program for the artistically gifted in your school or community, ask yourself these questions:

1. What do the talented students need that they are not receiving at this time?
2. How much time am I willing to devote to persuading the proper authorities to establish a program; to write a proposal?
3. If I win my case, would I be willing to turn the administrative reins over to others?

Keep in mind, too, that the support received is proportionate to the effort expended. If you are determined to get things going and committed to fulfilling the demands that will be made on you, then the chances are very good that you will be rewarded with a program.

Gifted children can benefit from work with posed models earlier than children of normal abilities. This applies to sculpture as well as drawing and painting. Drawing by ten-year-old, sculpture by twelve-year-old.

6 Funding: Who Pays?

One of the first things to consider in setting up a program for the artistically gifted is who is going to foot the bill. Money may be available at the school or district level, or you may have to seek out corporate, state, and federal sources. Securing funds is likely to require several of the qualities you expect in your gifted students: creativity, persistence, and mastery of technique — in this case, the technique of writing a clear, comprehensive, businesslike proposal is a skill of vital importance.

The Nonfunded School Level

Let us assume you are an art teacher with no school funding available for the program you have in mind. This can be discouraging, but remember that traditionally some of the best services rendered have involved no more than a concerned teacher.

What teachers can offer is largely themselves. One Miami teacher of the author's acquaintance has made it his business to seek out developing student artists among the Cuban refugee population. He has seen many of his students go on to pursue careers in art. Like many of his colleagues, he gives his time after school to meet with students. He also gives his weekends and evenings to accompany his students to gallery openings and art events, loans them books and magazines, and in every way possible demonstrates his support.

If there is no possibility of obtaining school funding, take a hard look at your program as it now exists and ask yourself the following questions:

- Can I present a plan to the principal in which a number of periods would be set aside for art instruction for an invitational group of gifted students?
- Have I convinced my colleagues that such a program merits the release of students from their classes once or twice a week?
- Have I organized my own branch of the National Art Honors Society so that those who should be are setting up exhibitions, planning field trips, scheduling speakers, and getting involved in other art activities?

- Can I meet with a few students after school hours on a weekly basis to review work, talk about art, or assign special projects?
- Is it legal in my system to charge fees? (This can be a critical issue in a photography program or in taking field trips.)

Minimal School Funding

At the next level funding comes from an in-house budget through the support of the principal. The many Advanced Placement art programs receive such funds for supplies or instructional materials that might not normally be available. (Advanced Placement students may be taught in separate classes or integrated into regular classes.) Since Advanced Placement already exists in the academic subjects, an Advanced Placement art class should not be surprising to a senior high school principal.

Before you approach your principal for funding, prepare an estimate of how many students you have in mind. According to most estimates gifted children average five percent of any given school population. You may have more or fewer; only your system of identification will tell you. (See chapter seven.) When you ask for funds for a specified number of students, have on hand the information that led you to arrive at that particular number. If you teach on the secondary level, and you are not the only art teacher, make your presentation with the complete art staff. Remember, it is easier to turn down one person who hasn't done his homework than it is to reject a committee that has all the facts in hand. This principle holds true at any level of the educational bureaucracy.

The District Level

At the district level the school superintendent, the school board, or the district art supervisor can be approached. All of these have some influence on how district monies are allocated. At this level, it is best to aim for a system-wide project open to all schools. The one to present the case for such a proposal should be the art supervisor with the support of the art staff. School boards may need to be persuaded since only a minority of the school population will be involved in the program, a minority that has never been given high priority.

Under the central plan, all students who are accepted might come to one location. Saturday morning is often a good time to meet since schools are not in use and money can sometimes be saved in custodial fees.

In one program the morning was divided into two one-and-a-half-hour sessions. Since there were two art rooms, four groups of twenty children were served. Charging a nominal fee of $1.50 per student per session netted $30 per class per morning, which paid the teachers. Additional costs (materials and custodial fees) were picked up by the school committee. As the program grew, the same plan allowed the center to add a primary age group and a drama group, which were not treated as programs for the gifted.

If district funding is not available, funds can be sought from the business community, the state arts council, the state department of education, or the Arts in Education program, the program of the U.S. Department of Education, ESEA, Title IX, Gifted and Talented Children's Act of 1978. This will require a proposal that can range from one to dozens of pages depending on the amount of money requested.

State Support

Support at the state level ranges from extensive (as in Illinois, Pennsylvania, Connecticut, and New York) to minimal. To determine how much support your state can offer, call your state department of education and ask to speak to the person in charge of special education and programs for the gifted.

Next find out who is employed by your system to write proposals and apply for grants. Make an appointment with this person and ask to see both the latest state or USDE guidelines. The proposal writer can interpret the publication if necessary and pinpoint the grant(s) best suited to your needs. Your state arts consultant can also alert you to other available government or private grants.

An understanding of guidelines will usually indicate the grade levels and purposes for which funding is available. (Some monies are awarded on a shared basis.) The applicant should then rough out a proposal, giving all information required, paying particular attention to the need or justification and the means of evaluation.

Your state arts council can put you on their mailing list and give you a list of the art organizations in your area that could be of service to you. The American Association of Architects, Artists Equity, The American Crafts Council, The Art Director's Club are all organizations that have helped art teachers in the past. They may not be able to donate funds, but they can probably offer services that can enrich your program.

Many states support such art centers as the Governor's School in North Carolina and the New York State program at Fredonia State University. The Florida Art Education Association offers three-day workshops as well as a year-round art center with live-in accommodations for students from ninth grade through the junior college level. Pennsylvania and Illinois also conduct active programs for the gifted. Even if support for your particular program is not available from your state, all state offices have specialists assigned to help develop programs for the gifted. In some cases these people work out of a special needs program.

Most city to state programs stress all of the arts and are for secondary level students. The rarest programs are those designed for the artistically gifted on the elementary level, although such programs are currently showing the fastest rate of growth.

The United States Department of Education

The Gifted and Talented Children's Education Program (Bill 84,080) of the U.S. Department of Education is the logical place to begin the search for federal funds. This serves certain categories of applicants and offers several levels of assistance. It also tells you what *cannot* be funded (construction, remodeling, stipends, transportation, meals, etc.). It distinguishes between state administered and discretionary grants, describes selection criteria for both, makes its awards on a point system based upon fulfillment of criteria, and sets deadlines. Since the awards range from $15,000 to $400,000 (averaging $62,000), we can assume that the planning involved in applying may take quite a bit of someone's unpaid time. (See the appendix for the complete form.)

Contour drawing provided the basis for this affectionate family portrait by a senior high student.

Corporate Funding

There are, of course, other sources of financial support. In Calgary, Alberta, and Miami, Florida, interested individuals from the business community have endowed special art programs and even set up foundations of various kinds.

Phillips Petroleum Corporation leads a group of corporations that works with the State Arts Council of Oklahoma; the result of this collaboration is the Quartz Mountain School for the gifted. (See the model program on page 111.)

Walt Disney studios founded an entire art school (California Institute of the Arts in Los Angeles). The General Motors Design Program pioneered career education for gifted high school students by bringing them to their design laboratories for brief periods of instruction. There are, therefore, many precedents for corporate support, particularly as it relates to career education. The NAEA (National Art Education Association) has published a series of four booklets on all aspects of career education (see the bibliography). Several references in these booklets are given for connecting your program to funding that already exists for the gifted. The field of career education is the latest to emerge as a priority area on both state and national levels and it is in education on art careers that the NAEA publication can be of practical use.

Guidelines for Seeking Financial Support

Finding financial support for your program requires careful planning. The task should be easier, though, if you keep the following points in mind:

Relate the Program to Your Community

Your program has a better chance of being supported if it relates to the nature of the funding organization or to the school/community. Be sensitive to how administrators and parents perceive the value and nature of art and be realistic in your attempt to heighten their consciousness. What can you offer the children of a community with high unemployment, with a high ratio of professionals, in a rural setting? Some connection should be made between your program and the social setting of the community. Businesses are sensitive to this consideration since their own welfare is tied to the community in which their employees live. Some communities may be particularly responsive to arguments which relate to general cultural aspirations and the psychological well-being of students.

Research Organizations' Funding Histories

If you are approaching foundations, philanthropies and corporations, find out where their money has been donated in the past. The simplest way to do this is to telephone an organization and ask for someone in public relations. This information may point you in the right direction before you even begin your planning.

Relate Money to Ideas

Bear in mind that you are not asking for money; you are selling an idea. Financial need should be treated as an incidental, not as a major matter. Your idea must be presented in a well-planned, soundly conceived proposal that is translated into fiscal terms in order to inform potential sponsors what the program will cost. By all means be as specific as you can; it is only natural for the sponsors to want to know how the money will be spent. As one administrator put it in an article, "Stalking the School Administrator," he wrote for *Art Education: Journal of the NAEA* (P.D. Houston, Sept. 1981):

> Unfortunately, the arts advocate too often approaches the school administrator using "art language" and not administrative language. Administrators tend to be illiterate to such terms as "esthetics," "feeling," "interrelating," or "self-expression." Administrative language is more locked into "per pupil costs," "cost effective," or "accountability" — harsh words, but ones based upon the reality of today's school management. The successful arts advocate will attempt to package ideas or proposals in these reality-based words. Also, the arts advocate should try to do as much preparation and brainwork on the program concept prior to the presentation to the administrator as is humanly possible. The less follow-up required of the administrator, the better.

Be realistic in your estimates and do not play the game of inflating figures on the assumption that they will automatically be cut. Be able to defend a budget on an item-by-item basis and have good reasons for everything you request.

Here are some of the costs that will have to be considered.

Administration
Administrator
Secretary
Office supplies, postage, flyers, posters, telephone
Refreshments for meetings
Guards at street corners
Custodians
Building fees
Insurance

Instruction
Teachers, aids
Honoraria for visiting artists
Honoraria for volunteers (students, parents)
Field trips
   Buses and drivers
In-service teacher education (workshops, lectures, conferences,
     study groups to develop curricula)

Supplies
Expendable
   Paints, paper, crayons, etc.
Equipment
   Potters' wheels, presses, brayers, cameras, etc.
Equipment maintenance
   Repairs before or after program
Books, reproductions
Rental
   Films, media equipment

Evaluation and Dissemination
Evaluator's fee
Printing costs
Documentation fee for photographer and other media specialists

This nine-year-old develops a schema with motifs from mythology, science fiction, and horror movies.

The monies you request should demonstrate that you can look ahead and anticipate emergencies and problems. If you have never made out a budget, seek help from someone in the school system with experience in this area. All systems have business managers; don't be afraid to use them.

Diversify Finally, plan for more than one source of support. Think of your program as a group of components, each of which can suggest different means of support. Art suppliers have often donated materials. For example, one manufacturer provides materials such as acrylic paints for the program for teenagers at Boston University. Space has been given in churches, stores not yet rented, grange halls, and, of course, schools. Salaries have been funded by educational institutions, businesses, and private donors.

Working within a school system, you can also become part of someone else's grant. Find out who already has a grant and see if they would be open to input from the visual arts. The most obvious place for you to be is in one of the many programs for the gifted that have not yet accommodated the arts. The majority of these grants are still used for the academically gifted only, and here is where your power of persuasion is most needed.

7 Identification: Who Will Be Served?

Many methods are possible in selecting the students to be served by a special art program. The choice depends mainly on what kind of program is planned. Before selection of individual students can take place, however, basic decisions must be made about the age and type of students to be included.

The Target Group

Deciding upon the grade level at the outset helps to focus all future decisions. Art theory can be incorporated in a program for junior high students, while it is not a likely inclusion in a program for early elementary children. If the class is on the senior high level, the curriculum could resemble a college freshman course, with reading and writing assignments and group discussions. It is even possible to offer a course in aesthetics or art criticism at this level. The Advance Placement courses in drawing, general studio, and art history provide a ready-made format from which to launch new programs.

Since giftedness can emerge at any age, it is difficult to state a case for serving one level over another unless, of course, practical considerations enter in, such as portfolio development and career preparation for older students.

Children of varying ages can be mixed, although certain boundaries set by the students themselves should not be ignored. Gifted children have a greater tolerance for mixed groupings than do most children, but seventeen-year-old twelfth graders still may not feel comfortable working next to thirteen-year-old seventh graders. Practical considerations will define the age level, too. Younger children may not be able to use public transportation for a community-based program.

In addition to the age, you may want to consider the nature of the talents of the students you want to attract. Most programs are general in nature and aim at the fine-arts-oriented child; creative problem-solving and historical/critical activities are used as adjuncts. The emphasis can just as easily be reversed with academic achievement placed in high priority and studio performance a secondary condition.

The target group, as well as the activities offered, may also be selected with the strengths of the instructor in mind. A teacher who is also a professional potter or printmaker might be most effective

A junior high school student studies her large-scale imaginative interpretation of a small photograph. Since this was a new direction for the artist, the vital process of risk taking was encouraged.

teaching his or her specialty, although many handle other areas with equal ease. You may also decide upon a particular group, such as lower elementary, simply because it has been ignored in the past. If you decide to become a part of another program, in all probability the age group will already have been decided for you. In general, teachers are apt to promote students on the level in which they teach, while supervisors tend to include the full range of ages.

Methods of Identification

The method of identifying the students to be included in a special art program varies with the size of the population to be tapped. A teacher who has to choose sixteen students from six or seven art classes for an after school art club has an easier task than a supervisor who must select students from an entire city-wide system for a program. Since facilities are usually limited, some process of sifting students must be used.

There are several ways to select students.

1. A selective system uses some method of screening to identify the students to be accepted. This is a condition that will apply to any situation that depends upon grants.
2. A nonselective system accepts everyone who applies, but after observing the behavior and the artwork of the entire group, separates the high achievers. Teachers in the Dade County system, which is based on nonselective admission, have found that some students discover their potential only in a controlled atmosphere with peers who take art seriously. Underachievers are either turned away or taught in another class on the understanding that the advanced group is open to them if and when they show certain required evidence of improvement. In any case, all applicants must be told at the very outset the conditions of and reasons for policy.
3. A self-selective system explicitly lists all the requirements in advance so that the students, their parents, and teachers can decide whether they think the program is worth the effort that will have to be expended.

This section is primarily concerned with selective systems.

The characteristics of gifted children were sketched in Part I. For the most part, teachers usually feel they have a clear picture of the students who should be involved in a special program. Although informal teacher judgment is still the most prevalent form of identification, it is rarely considered adequate when grant monies are involved. The more precise the selection technique, the more the target group will fit the goals of the program.

Program administrators are not always looking for well-rounded students, but they do want well-rounded pictures of the students before making admissions decisions. Bear in mind, however, that the more complete the student records, the more expensive and time-consuming the screening process.

The following selection methods use tests for the various modes of intelligence (cognitive, creative, and artistic), referrals, and other techniques. I.Q. and other standardized tests are only touched on since these are part of established educational practice and on record in the guidance office.

Nonart Means of Identification

No program reviewed by the author uses all the tests described below. The tests described provide a range of investigation. It is wide enough for an adequate basis on which to choose the kind of student you want to attract.

Tests for Scholastic Ability

Screening often begins with a look at general scholastic ability as determined on such tests as the IOWA Tests of Basic Skills (grades 9 through 12), the Metropolitan Achievement Tests (grades 1 through 12), and the Stanford-Binet I.Q. Scale. Sixteen or so of these tests are most generally used. (See the appendix for the names and addresses of several frequently consulted tests.) In the writer's opinion, Scholastic Achievement, I.Q., and similar tests should *not* be used as a *major* criteria in screening for an art program because the correlation between academic achievement and artistic ability is unclear.

The New Rochelle program in New York State (see page 103) requires high performance in both art and academic domains; the Warminster, Pennsylvania programs require an I.Q. score of 130 or more for admission. Suburban school systems with higher income levels tend to place more value on nonart abilities than do lower-income urban communities, which are more likely to value the social benefits to be derived from special programs. The requirements for admission to special programs in lower-income areas are usually, in order of importance:

1. A strong desire to attend the program
2. Strong interest in visual expression
3. Academic achievement
4. Scores on I.Q. tests

Tests for Creative Thinking

Tests for creative thinking are given by a teacher to all students in a class. The focus here is not on attitudes, but on how well children can solve problems and use their imaginations. Such tests may be verbal or figural, that is, require some drawing activity, although drawing skill is not being tested. Paul Torrance, a leading scholar in the field of creativity, uses product improvement as one of several exercises. The following assignments are typical.

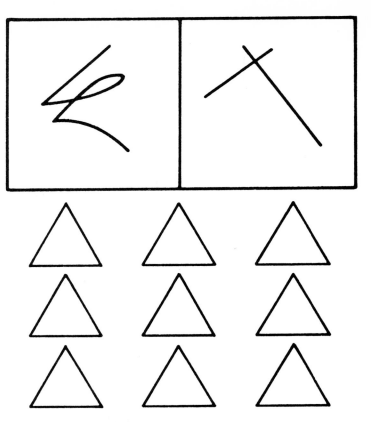

Torrance Tests of Thinking Creatively with Pictures. Personnel Press, Inc. Princeton, New Jersey 08540.

- By adding lines to the figures, you can sketch some interesting objects or pictures. Try to think of some picture or object that no one else will think of. Try to make it tell as complete and as interesting a story as you can by adding to and building up your first idea. Make up an interesting title for each of your drawings and write it at the bottom of each block next to the number of the figure.
- In the middle of a page sketch a stuffed toy rabbit of the kind you can buy in most dime stores for about one or two dollars. It is about six inches tall and weighs six ounces. List the cleverest, most interesting and unusual ways you can think of to change this toy rabbit so that children will have more fun playing with it. Do not worry about how much the changes will cost. Think only about what would make it more fun to play with as a toy.

Other questions in this category could read:

- Describe all the uses for a simple object such as a brick.
- Here are six pictures. How well can you connect them with a story?
- A man comes out of a plane with a bulging briefcase. He has a worried expression on his face. Write down everything you can about the person that makes a connection between what he is carrying and his state of mind.

Although these questions require written responses, spelling, grammar, and punctuation are not as important as the ideas being conveyed.

In all of these tasks, there is no right or wrong answer. However, some solutions will be more detailed and complex, and offer more surprises than others. These are the factors upon which Torrance's scoring system is based.

Torrance has also developed techniques for identifying talent among disadvantaged students. From his work with students from poor minority backgrounds, Torrance has concluded that a test can create or destroy a "psychological atmosphere" that can influence a child's score. Care should therefore be taken that the content of any test is not heavily slanted toward a culture to which some children may not feel a part. This could include assumptions regarding the nature of families, vacations, reading, and activities based on middle-and upper-economic life-styles.

Peer Identification

Although research shows that peer identification is not completely reliable, it can help identify children who are reticent about their abilitites and who may have revealed their talents more openly to their classmates than to adults. This belief applies to nonart as well as to art behavior.

The sample questions that follow lead students to identify creative classmates. Imagination, the ability to speculate and to play with ideas, is often revealed through students' observation of each other both in and out of school. The questions to be asked students at the secondary level deal with attitudes and personal preferences. These questions are taken from "Helping Teachers Teach, Teaching the Gifted and Talented," a publication of the Minnesota Education Association.

Peer Identification of Creativity, Elementary Level
Pretend our class found a puppy on the playground.

1. Which three students would be most likely to think up lots of names for the puppy?
   Which three would make up the most *unusual* names?
   Which three would probably come up with the name we would finally decide on?

2. Which three students would be most likely to write a story about the puppy?
3. If we designed a collar for our puppy, which three students would probably come up with the *most* designs for the collar?

Peer Identification of Creativity, Secondary Level
Think about the students in our class. Answer the following questions as completely as possible.

1. Which three students are the most curious about many things?
2. Have the most ideas and solutions to problems?
3. Like to take chances?
4. Have the most fun imagining situations and things?
5. Have the best sense of humor?
6. Are individualists?
7. Are apt to question authority?

Rating of Multiple Abilities   A comprehensive scale that rates both "thinking and feeling" characteristics for secondary students was devised by Frank Williams. This instrument is based on eight factors of behavior that can be observed, each of which has six characteristics worth noting. Peer identification is used. A general characteristic is stated, and the students are asked to identify by name the classmate who best fulfills the descriptions that fall under each category.

Since space does not permit inclusion of the complete test, examples from each category have been selected. If you are interested in having the full set, write to The Williams Cognitive Affective Interaction Model, Total Creativity Kit, Education Technology Publications, Inc., 140 Sylvan Avenue, Englewood Cliffs, N.J. 07632.

1. The student is a *fluent* thinker:
   The student who thinks of a number of answers when a question is asked.
   The student who draws several pictures when asked to draw only one.
2. The student is a *flexible* thinker:
   The student who thinks of various ways to use an object other than its common use.
   The student who can apply a principle or concept in subjects other than the one in which it was introduced.

3. The student is an *original* thinker:

   The student who likes objects placed off-center in a room or prefers asymmetry in drawings and designs.

   The student who is a nonconformist and cannot help being different by having a new twist in thinking about things.

4. The student is an *elaborative* thinker:

   The student who will add lines, color, and details to a drawing.

   The student who senses a deeper meaning to an answer or solution by producing more detailed steps.

5. The student is *curious* and *inquisitive* by nature:

   The student who continually explores books, games, maps, pictures, etc.

   The student who needs no real push to explore something unfamiliar and exploration is a natural part of his or her behavior.

6. The student is *imaginative* and can *visualize* or dream about things that have never happened to him or her:

   The student who can see things in a picture or drawing that no one else has seen.

   The student who can wonder about something that has never happened.

7. The student is *complex* by nature and likes to tackle difficult problems or tasks:

   The student who wants to figure things out for himself or herself without help.

   The student who seeks more difficult answers rather than accepting an easy one.

8. The student is *courageous* and a *risk taker*, not afraid of failure or criticism:

   The students who will admit to a mistake or failure.

   The student who prefers to take a chance or dare just to see where it will take him or her.

The Interview   The interview, while rarely used as a sole criteria for selection, nevertheless provides insights that cannot be obtained through an examination of art work. Interviews can be conducted on a one-to-one basis, or by a group of people. They are used largely in secondary programs where relatively few students are screened for national or state recognition. In January the Arts Recognition Talent Search (ARTS) committee interviews thirty candidates for four Pres-

A ninth-grader shows imaginative reconstruction in her two-color block print through combining human and animal forms.

idential Scholar awards. In the spring, interviewers for state programs, such as those run by Georgia, Florida, and North Carolina, speak personally to their top level of applicants.

An interview can be useful in determining a student's ideas and attitudes toward art. It is based on the assumption that the element of human interaction will encourage a flow of feelings and thoughts that might not normally appear on paper.

A predetermined set of questions indicates a *directive* approach, but this should be combined with *nondirective* approaches that allow occasional deviations from the set questions. The interviewer is there to listen to what may lie beneath the surface of a self-conscious and uncomfortable teenager's conversation. The Arts Recognition and Talent Search (ARTS) conducts fifteen minute interviews with each candidate. Most of the conversation centers around examples of art work which students are required to display. The examining committee is very much aware of how discomforting such an experience can be, but feels that nothing can relax one more than discussing one's own work. During the course of conversation topics may emerge such as artistic influences, plans for the future, and personal opinions on art related topics.

Since a record of the interview is necessary, the interviewer will have to take notes or use a tape recorder. Either technique may be temporarily uncomfortable for the student, but self-consciousness usually disappears as the interviewer establishes that he or she is really on the student's side. Tapes are handy to use in comparing one candidate with another and in sharing perceptions with fellow judges.

One of the most thorough interview systems has been developed by the state of Georgia for its Governor's Honors Program. One form has four questions dealing with art knowledge and skills and the other form has six questions that cover attitudes about art. The former is graded on a point system and the latter sets up statements that the interviewer rates on a five-point scale from strongly disagree (1) to strongly agree (5). The statements deal with the applicant's ability to exhibit personal maturity, genuine desire to participate, positive attitudes toward art and artists, evidence of interest and involvement in school and community activities, open-mindedness toward artistic experimentation, and the general overall impression received by the interviewer. Since the form for assessing knowledge and skills is extensive, it has been included in the appendix.

Art-Centered Identification

Self-evaluation: The Wilson Cognitive Instrument

With the instrument developed by Brent and Marjorie Wilson, we begin to assess art aptitudes in elementary children. This test requires drawing tasks as well as statements of attitudes about art. While it relies on student identification, it is considerably more precise than similar tests. The Wilsons devised this test after a nine-year study of artistically gifted children. Sample questions are given under four divisions: opinions and attitudes on ability, artists, time, and imagination. All statements are checked against a five-point scale ("strongly agree, agree, undecided, disagree, strongly disagree").

The following samples have been selected from the Wilsons' instrument. If you are interested in using the entire set, contact the authors at the Department of Art Education, Pennsylvania State University, University Park, PA 16802.

ABILITY
I draw much better than most of the kids my age.
    Strongly agree
    Agree
    Undecided
    Disagree
    Strongly disagree
Talent in art is not a very important thing to have.
My friends are always asking me to draw things for them.

ARTIST
I would love to meet some famous artists and find out how to be-
come an artist myself.
Wanting to be an artist is not a very good thing.

TIME
It's not good to spend a lot of time drawing and making art.
Many times I would rather draw by myself than play with my
friends.
When I can't make a drawing look the way I want it to, I do it again
and again until it comes out right.

IMAGINATION
I am always using my imagination and doing such things as dream-
ing up stories and planning drawings.
It's bad for kids to daydream and to picture imaginary things in their
minds.
Quickly draw sketches for ideas that you might like to make into
paintings. Try to make each sketch unusual and make each one different from the others. Put lots of detail in each sketch. Imagine that
you are standing in the middle of a street looking into the distance.
There are buildings on both sides of the street. Draw the street and
the buildings as they would look to you.
In the four frames, draw a story. The story may be about a person,
an animal, plants or insects, cars or planes, an imaginary character,
or any other thing you would like. In the story, show something ex-
citing or dangerous happening, what happens next, and how things
finally turn out.
Draw a person who has just kicked a ball very, very hard. Try to
show all of the action in the body, arms, and legs.
The artist Leonardo da Vinci wrote:

> If you wish to make an animal imagined by you to appear natural —
> let us say a dragon — then take for its head that of a hound, with the
> eyes of a cat, the ears of a porcupine, the nose of a greyhound, the
> brow of a lion, the temples of an old rooster, and the neck of a water
> tortoise.

Draw your own imaginary animal by combining lots of parts from
many different animals. Make your imaginary animal as detailed as
you can.

National Art Assessment of Educational Progress: Art Objectives

Brent Wilson has also developed another means of identifying the talented: the National Assessment of Art Test. This test is part of an investigation into all areas of the curriculum to ascertain the degrees of learning among selected age groups (9-17 yrs.) in every region of the U.S. The art section is based upon a series of questions and tasks selected from the recommendations of leading art educators. Although this test is not intended to be used for identifying the gifted, it does provide some useful guidelines for studying student work. It deals with the student's ability to:

1. Perceive and respond to aesthetic elements in art
   Age 9   Identify themes of specific works of art.
   Age 13   Translate the meaning of conventional symbols commonly depicted in works of art.
   Age 17   Describe how the treatment of the theme or idea of two or more works of art is similar or different.
2. Value art as a realm of experience
   Age 9   Observe aesthetic objects in natural and man-made environments.
   Age 13   Produce art during leisure time.
   Age 17   Belong to art organizations.
3. Produce works of art
   All ages   Produce an imaginative work of art, such as an animal or other object that looks like no other object has looked before.
   Age 9   Produce a work of art with a particular mood, feeling, or expressive character.
   Age 13   Produce a work (landscape, city, or town) that has a particular feeling such as coolness, loneliness, warmness, wetness, or spookiness.
   Age 17   Produce a work of art that has a particular composition such as vertical, horizontal, diagonal concentric, symmetrical, and asymmetrical; that uses deep or shallow space; or that has an open or closed composition.
4. Know about art
   Age 9   Recognize well-known works of art.
   Age 13   Select the statement that best characterizes the significance of a work of art.
   Age 17   Explain why certain key works are considered to be important to the history of art.

5. Form reasoned, critical judgments about the significance and quality of works of art
Age 9   Judge a work of art on the basis of how well its various aspects relate to each other.
Age 13   Judge a work of art on the basis of how well the artist has utilized the inherent qualities of a particular medium.
Age 17   Judge a work of art on the basis of how successfully it expresses aspects of the society in which it was produced.

Its results can go so far as to tell one how a twelve-year-old rural Southern child draws the human figure in comparison to the same age child in a Midwestern urban city. Since it is not designed to reveal the gifted, the one who uses it would have to decide upon the level of scoring that would qualify a child for the program in question. The test is the most comprehensive in nature of its kind, but could be used selectively for specific purposes.

For full information write to Brent Wilson at the Department of Art Education, Pennsylvania State University, University Park, PA 16802.

Clearly Art-Centered Identification

As we move more directly into the sphere of artwork, we find fewer screening instruments from which to choose. Perhaps this is because art teachers find it awkward to place their normal mode of operation into the form of a test. Art teachers, however, are constantly making judgments since criticism of some sort lies at the heart of instruction. When students begin to work, the teacher moves about the room encouraging, commenting, offering suggestions. Occasionally, the teacher is struck by the consistency of outstanding work by two or three students. If a program for the gifted is begun and the teacher is asked to help design some formal means of identifying the high producers, the teacher must stop and ask, "What is it exactly that these students are doing that catches my attention? What sets them apart?"

Such teachers would have little trouble deciding which of their students to admit to a special art class in their own school, but suppose the students want to apply to a program outside the school? Someone is going to have to set up a screening process. The teacher in us tells us to study attitudes and work habits; the artist in us bids

An example of strong memory. The handling of detail, space, and action places this nine-year-old girl well ahead of her peers. The quality of the line (loose, free, and searching) also sets her apart.

us to study the student's work. Both sides should be heeded. The "Production Strengths" and "Learning Strengths" sections of the Kenmore Personal Characteristics Appraisal Instrument (see Appendix) are particularly concerned with artistic behavior.

In *The Artist in Each of Us* (Pantheon Books, 1951), one of the few sources for case histories of talented children, Florence Cane discusses the progress of five children from childhood through adolescence. As Director of Art for the Counseling Centre for Gifted Children of New York University she was involved with children with special aptitudes in art as far back as the early 1930s. Portfolios of students recommended by teachers were submitted and Cane responded by commenting on such factors as movement, dynamics, organization, and spirit. If she was impressed by the high overall level of the work submitted, the student was accepted, in most cases with a full scholarship. Once admitted, the nature of her reports changed. They then moved beyond the work to the nature of the student, always searching for links between work and personality. As an example, when first reviewing the portfolio of Harold A., Cane used such descriptive phrases as "high quality of imagination," "strong power in the concept," and "good feeling of space, distance, and design." In her later reports, Cane concentrated upon Harold and noted he was "sensitive, kindly, thoughtful of others, eager to learn."

Although some teachers now try to consider in advance the very characteristics that Cane dealt with *after* Harold A. was selected, the virtues of personality mentioned above still rarely figure in admis-

The thirteen-year-old girl who drew this has already grasped the relation of wholes to parts; a loose, searching line invests her work with freshness.

This tenth grader's monochromatic watercolor wash study sensitively combines elements of both drawing and painting.

sion processes. The problem of personality and attitudes (as in Harold's case) is usually kept apart from the state of the art product.

Tasks can be designed to determine what a student is capable of doing based upon his past experience while other tasks can tell us how the student functions in a totally new situation. The activities that follow are means of identification that could also be assigned in a program. They reveal specific studio behaviors, and may indicate a wider range of skills than is usually dealt with in the average class. They are largely the writer's suggestions and art teachers can review their own curricula for examples of activities that can lend themselves to judgment on any scale that extends from below average to outstanding performance. This set can be used from the sixth grade through junior high school, although some problems are appropriate for senior high school students as well. Grading is on a four-point scale.

ART-CENTERED TASKS

Observational Ability
From memory, draw a seated person.
The teacher should review or present the process of contour line drawing. Then working from the posed model, have the students draw the seated person a second time.
(Judge for range of improvement or for quality of drawing as an independent effort: handling of detail, quality of line, placement on paper, etc.)

Color Sensitivity
Write a phrase or word on the blackboard (e.g., "a sense of desolation," or "the happiest time of my life"). Ask the students to produce a painting based upon the phrase avoiding the use of any recognizable subjects.
(Judge for range of color and its appropriateness to the topic. You can have a separate division for composition, but that is much more difficult than sensitive use of color.)

Ability to Fuse Drawing and Imagination
Tell a story using only drawings. Convey this in a comic book format using no more than twenty-four frames.
(Judge for narrative invention and the ability to create forms that make meaning clear.)

Emotional Expressiveness
Using two human figures as vehicles for emotional expression, create a composition based upon a word with strong associations such as "aggression," "rage," or "love." This exercise should have two media phases: one clay, the other paint or drawing.
(Judge for the appropriateness of the treatment to the subject and for sensitive use of media.)

Memory
Have the group study a still life or some other observable subject (posed figure, a painting, or a slide of a landscape will do). Remove the subject from the students and have them draw as much as they can recall.
(Do not judge for technique, originality, or sensitivity to media, but

simply for the number of objects included and the accurateness of their relationship to each other.)

Imaginative Re-creation
Have the students close their eyes as you describe a scene in great detail. Then have them execute this mind picture as they see it in felt pen or pen and ink and watercolor.
(This task should be judged largely for detail and composition, but handling of media can also be considered.)

Handling of Space
Explain the meaning of the words "close-up," "middle ground," and "background." Review the story of "Noah's Ark" and ask the students to illustrate it in pencil.
(Judge for the numbers of devices used to place objects in space and for the use of the three terms used above.)

Sensitivity of Media
Have the students draw from observations a "shish kabob" consisting of a ball of yarn, a ping pong ball, and a half-eaten apple, all impaled on a long stick or knitting needle.
(Judge for sensitive use of pencil to indicate change of surface textures.)
Create a design based upon the initials of your name and paint it in flat tones using tempera.

With ten tasks, each rated from a low of one point to a high of four, the completed scores should look as follows:

Exceptional:	40 points
Above average:	30 points
Average:	20 points
Below average:	10 points

After grading the tests you must decide where your cutoff point will be. Any score above 30 in this example should be acceptable, but limited enrollment could require an even higher cutoff score.

Judging and Scoring
In assessing the artwork of an applicant, one problem is to get sensitive judges who have looked at a great deal of children's work. Then

be certain that the judges are looking for similar qualities so that reasonable agreement (one point of difference) is assured. The best way to accomplish this is to spend time on the training of judges. One method is to lay out a random sampling of at least a dozen pieces of work and then begin jointly sorting them by categories (1, 2, 3, 4). While the extreme ends of any scale are relatively easy to agree upon, the middle ground will bring about some debate. These discussions, however, are vital because it is here that judges must clearly articulate their views. The process of defending one's scores clarifies thinking.

Centrally Conducted Examinations   Some programs require students from a wide area to come to a central location for screening. This system has two advantages. Through personal interviews the judges have an opportunity to meet the applicants and learn firsthand their feelings and ideas about art. Such topics as favorite artists, the work of artists, and the students' own work can be discussed. Attitudes, knowledge, and personal enthusiasm about art can thus be quickly assessed.

Through studio activity the students can be observed working completely divorced from teacher influence. Judges can tailor studio activities to the examination area (e.g., "design an image for a wall of this room"). They can also give each participant the same set of materials (a box, some string, a ping pong ball, glue, and a box of toothpicks) and require the same tasks such as a self-portrait or a still life. Judges can decide upon the time allotted, the technique or media used, the kind of visual thinking considered significant. Above all, there will be no doubt that the work that emerges is the students' own.

Using Test Results   The results of art-centered methods of identification are of use even after the class has been selected. They can provide a teacher an overview of the level of competence of the group, as well as the general ability of individual students. The material can also be used diagnostically to point out each student's strengths and weaknesses. This last use can save precious class time by eliminating the need to test the students to assess particular abilities.

The classroom environment should provide an atmosphere conducive to learning in art. The room should be stimulating without being distracting and should reflect changes in the curriculum.

8 Curriculum: What Shall Be Taught?

Little information is available on the curricula of programs for the gifted in art. Of the several dozen program descriptions studied by the author, no more than two or three actually described the day-to-day activities. Information on goals and identification, on the other hand, were freely dealt with and often in great detail. The lack of information on activities is probably based on the assumption that it is the children, not the curricula, that make the difference in these programs.

This assumption commonly leads to two views on what should be taught. In the first case, the work level is simply advanced. College-level assignments are offered to senior high school students, senior high work to junior high students, and so forth. In the second case, standard grade level curricula are offered but with improved instruction, materials, and work conditions. It is difficult to recommend one approach over another. To simply move the same set of problems to a lower level may be a simplistic solution if the teachers of a higher level have little knowledge of the students or of the goals of the program. And having more money for equipment, space, and reduced class size will not amount to much if the level of instruction is mundane and uninspired. Obviously, gifted students need optimum conditions if they are to advance to the level which they are capable of reaching. The issues which follow reflect the many decisions that must be dealt with in creating such conditions.

Free Choice Versus Structure

Before a program can be developed, its initiators need to decide whether the curriculum will be planned or based on individual choice. In a free choice program the students choose their own activities. A student may work in clay one day and paint the next, moving from one material center to another, or the student may choose to do nothing at all. The danger here is that the group as a whole never enjoys the advantage that special preparation on the part of the teacher can provide. Why bother with a special film, a guest speaker, or a demonstration of a new material when everyone is off in a separate world? In the planned approach the teacher has a clear idea of the ends to be achieved and plans the activities accordingly. The objectives may center on the development of perceptual skills or of facility with certain media. Whatever the focal point, the students should be expected to become involved in tasks assigned in a certain sequence. In the most ideal programs, students have choices within the boundaries of clearly stated goals, and the teacher makes key instructional decisions and elicits high levels of concentration and hard work from the students.

Goals and Objectives

Assuming a structured approach has been chosen, another matter must be settled. Those setting up the program need to define what it is they hope the program will accomplish. In doing this, two types of purposes become evident: *goals* and *objectives*.

A goal is broader than an objective and concerns itself with the overall effect a program is meant to have, the general underlying intention. An objective is more specific. It is a subdivision of a goal and describes which particular skills are to be developed through the program. Any number of objectives may fall under a single goal.

Some examples of broad goals and objectives might be:

1. *Goal*   To prepare secondary school students to make more informed career decisions.
   Objective   To give the students a firsthand acquaintance with a minimum of a dozen artists in the artists' work environments.
2. *Goal*   To use community resources such as museums, historical societies, and architectural monuments in extending junior high school students' knowledge of art history.
   Objective   To so plan that students make on-site visits to locations of artistic significance, and to speak personally to some person asociated with each institution.
3. *Goal*   To use the gifts of underprivileged children to move them out of negative learning environments.
   Objective   To have records of students available for discussion with parents, so that future plans can be considered.
4. *Goal*   To dispel sexual and social stereotypes.
   Objective   To include artworks by men and women and various ethnic groups when presenting or discussing art history.

Two treatments of problem-solving in art history by senior high school students. The Michelangelo study is fractured, while Bronzino's approach is applied to a self-portrait.

5. *Goal* To instill improved work habits, a sense of responsibility, and seriousness about art in the students.
   Objective To require students to use a sketchbook as a matter of habit.

As goals and objectives are stated, a curriculum begins to take shape. A broad goal establishes what we hope a program will accomplish while an objective leads us to think about how the goal will be reached. The next stage is to further break down objectives into specific activities.

An outline of a curriculum at this stage might read:

BROAD GOAL To expand the talents of gifted junior high school students in activities that go beyond representational drawing.

OBJECTIVE 1 To develop facility in rendering surface and texture

TASK Impale several objects with sharply contrasting surfaces (an eggshell, a ball of twine, an orange, a piece of fur, for example) on a knitting needle. Convey the changing quality of the surface objects through control of the medium (pencil, charcoal, conté crayon, pen and ink, etc.).

OBJECTIVE 2   To use drawing skill for imaginative tasks

TASK A   After careful study of human and animal anatomy, create your own mythological figure embodying the physical elements of a bird, a mammal, and a human.

TASK B   Using a microscope, render a sample of cellular life form as carefully as you can. Turn your sketch into a fantasy landscape.

OBJECTIVE 3   To use drawing skill in problem-solving

TASK   Suppose you are on a team of planners trying to sell your city on a children's park. The year is 2300 A.D. and you are trying to create a nostalgic park environment reminiscent of the third quarter of the twentieth century. Through a series of quick sketches, indicate the kinds of structures you want to include. Make a layout, without details, to show their location and relation to each other.

Essential Activities

Several activities should be basic to a studio-centered program for the artistically gifted, no matter what the age level. Keep these activities in mind as you plan your curriculum.

Outside Assignments

Students in special art programs are not only prepared but eager to take on outside assignments, whether viewing an exhibition, a film, or TV show, reading selected material, keeping a sketchbook, or completing work begun in class. (It is not a bad idea to require *all* of the above from secondary students in grades 7 through 12.)

Linkage with Art History

There is not an activity you can plan that does not suggest some reference to art history, past or present. Teachers often agree with this in principle, but somehow don't get around to history or theory in class. The teacher of the gifted must find the time and means to use the students' studio experience to extend their knowledge of art history, theory, criticism, and even aesthetics.

Group Critique

Students should participate in group critiques at certain appropriate times during the course of the program. It is during such sessions

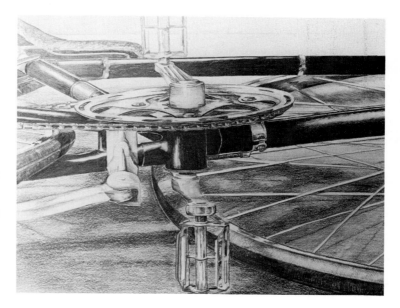

The unusual angle of the subject flattens the image and adds an interesting dimension to this blow-up of a segment of a bicycle by an eleventh-grade student.

that teachers can gain some inkling of the students' understanding of art terminology through their ability to articulate their ideas. Participation in group critiques teaches students to distance themselves from their emotions and to be more objective in viewing their own work. Critiques may be based upon the work of students or professional artists.

Keeping a Record
Each student should keep a portfolio of all work done in and outside of the classroom. Each work should be dated so that progress can be noted during periodic personal interviews and reviews, which should be a part of any program.

Participation in Evaluation
The students should be prepared to participate in evaluating the program at its conclusion. On the other hand, teachers and administrators should take student evaluations seriously, and use them for program improvement.

Participation in Final Exhibition
Students and teachers should plan together an exhibition for the conclusion of the course, deciding upon the location, the general theme, and the style of display. All aspects of an official opening should also be worked out. Artwork and written information are the basic components, but photo documentation, a continuous slide presentation, or a video tape could portray the program in action. A multivisual record of the program itself moves beyond the usual array of nicely matted artwork and conveys the flow of events and the ambiance of the program. Because the final presentation is in itself a learning experience, it is considered part of the curriculum. It can also be used by evaluators when assessing the whole program.

Stretching the Student

Observation, sensitivity to media, and the improvement of technique are the most commonly stressed skills in programs for artistically gifted students, particularly on the secondary level. The problem with this emphasis lies in the limited view of art it can give. Too much stress on skills can breed intolerance to new ways of working and foster premature specialization. While it is always advisable to begin with the immediately familiar world of students, it should be understood that, at some point, the students will be asked to move from the known to the unknown, from the familiar to the new.

The following sequence by the senior high level is an example of how the author led the students into a totally different realm of artistic thinking. The unit proceeded by gradual phases that the class found acceptably challenging.

UNIT TITLE   "The Self within Me"
BROAD GOAL   "To demonstrate how ideas and art problems progress from a single source — the human skeleton."

OBJECTIVE 1   Realistic portrayal of known objects

First session   Review of contour line drawing method
TASK   Draw objects, hands, posed costumed figures, and still life.

Second session   Contour line drawing continued
TASK   Make an enlarged line drawing of the human skeleton in soft pencil.

Third session   Review of techniques of shading, creating a range from dark to light, using gradation of pressure and cross-hatching
TASK   Isolate any three sections of the skeleton with squares or circles. Select any three colored pencils and add shading to lend dimensional quality.

OBJECTIVE 2   To design with known objects

Fourth session   Review of relevant design terminology
TASK   Place a large (12" x 18") sheet of tracing paper over the drawn skeleton. Move the paper about, seeing the forms as elements of design and connecting them to achieve a sense of coherency. Try two or three. When the desired composition is attained,

transfer the drawing from tracing paper to a sheet of white paper or mounting board.

Fifth session   Review of basic color theory through its terminology (value, complementary, analogous, warm, cool, etc.)

TASK   Using acrylic or tempera paint, turn the design into a hard-edge painting in a color system of each student's choice. Colors must be flat, clean, and unbroken.

OBJECTIVE 3   To express a concept

Sixth and seventh sessions   Discussion of the nature of collage and assemblage

TASK   Create an assemblage in a container (cigar box, hat box, violin case, etc.) and make a statement about life and death by relating the selected items, their colors and textures. (Teacher's statement: "For ten hours you have been dealing with a real human skeleton. Don't tell me you have not been speculating about the meaning of death — and of life. Now tell me what you thought by the way you select and arrange objects. Forget the scientific specimen on the table. Now go inside yourself and see what you find.")

OBJECTIVE 4   To note how work on a large scale alters the effect of drawing. To use "line" in a different context.

Eighth session   Creating a mural

TASK   Brown mural paper is placed on one wall and patches of black paper and newspaper are pasted on in a rough collage. Each student picks up a bone and returns to the first lesson — a line drawing of an observed object. Colors are of the students' choosing, the only rule being that the color changes as it moves from one part of the collage to another. When each bone has been drawn in paint, transitional forms have to be created to give the mural a sense of flow.

The sequence of the eight sessions described above effected a transition from skills of representation to inner responses, and in the course of the unit dealt with problems in design and color theory. Each phase had its own set of referents from the history of art (Da Vinci for *realistic portrayal*, Joseph Cornell for *assemblage,*

Picasso and Matisse for *line*, Ingres for *shading*, etc.). Each phase had its own set of concepts, its own vocabulary. Any session or phase could have functioned as a separate project. It was the grouping, the ordering of experience, that made the difference.

Specific Activities

While no course of study for the artistically gifted is publicly available, the Advanced Placement program in General Studio and Drawing has published a suggested list of activities. Since the committee that made out the list is composed of respected artists and art educators, it has been included for reference. Although it was prepared for senior high school students with college credit in mind, many of the problems are suitable for elementary and junior high levels; these have been designated by the letters *E* and *JH*. The author has also regrouped the activities according to the concept emphasized, and has added a number of his own suggestions (marked with asterisks).

In choosing activities for a particular level, remember that while most activities can be made more complex for more advanced ages, the reverse may not hold true. Many of the activities, especially those listed under the observations category, are appropriate for all students.

Observation

- Work with still lifes, figures, self-portraits, objects, landscapes, and groups of people with some sharply focused objective in mind, such as a concentration upon texture, depth, or range of tones.   V-SH
- Make studies of everyday or exotic objects: feet, shoes, twigs, animal skulls, weapons, tools, rope knots, paper bags, machine parts. Take a whole object such as a piece of popcorn, or a section of complex object, such as a bicycle, and blow it up ten times in size.   E, JH
- Portray multiple views of the same subject, such as a toy truck. E, JH
- Use all-white still lifes based on geometric forms (a painted rubber ball, a milk carton) for exercises in value, tonality, and light. Use such techniques as soft tonal gradation and cross-hatching.   JH

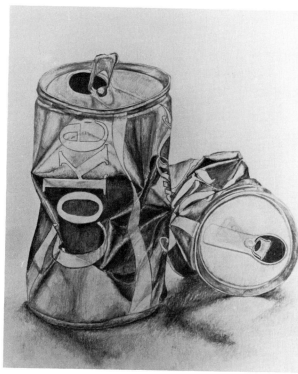

The mastery of texture is gained through the study of objects. Here beer cans and paper bags are crisply executed by a senior high school student who displays observational skills and a sensitive use of media.

The study of a single object from many points of view appears in many western curricula. The pine cone segment is studied through line, tone, and texture by a South African student.

Four approaches to the self-portrait: The first two, although varying in style, are basically conventional in nature. The other two demand a more active response from the viewer.

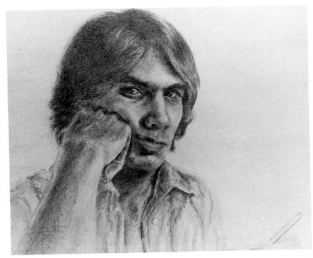

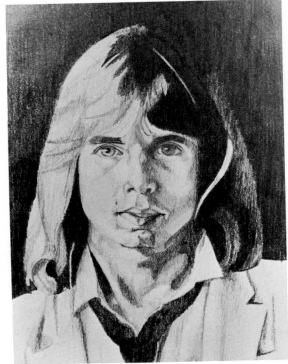

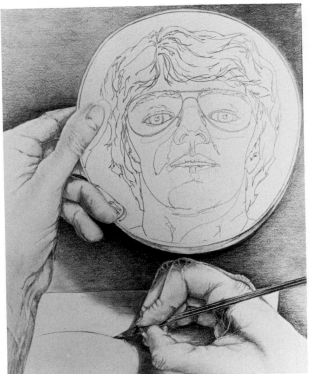

- Use the art room as an object, working for spaces between objects, perhaps articulating space by connecting easels, chairs, and ceiling with colored yarn; figures may or may not be included.   JH
- Integrate human figures in a still life background; other subjects could include bones, plant life, portions of the body, drapery, landscape, and crumpled paper.   JH
- Study the human figure to reveal the sympathetic relationship between the surface and the underlying forms. Exercises should emphasize gesture, economy of means, descriptive contour based upon nuance of line.   JH

Development of Media Skill

- Blow-ups: Each student receives a small square that is a part of a complex composition of a painting, photograph, or drawing and blows it up, exploring a wide range of tones; all segments are then assembled into a mural-sized version. While the exercise lends itself to several uses, here it should emphasize a particular technique or media.   E, JH
- Execute a bas-relief, either monochromatic or multicolored. Any of several techniques could be used, including sculpture or inkless embossing.   E, JH
- The instructor could arrange a demonstration of less commonly used media, such as egg tempera, scratchboard, silverpoint, rubbings, and encaustic.   E, JH
- Write your name backwards and upside down for pure motor control. A related exercise is drawing one hand with the other.   JH
- Make a print using a relatively difficult printing technique, such as soft ground, aquatint, lift ground, and mixed-print media including photo techniques. Basic techniques (line etching or drypoint for example) are not appropriate in this problem.   JH
- Copy exemplary works for improvement in a particular area.   JH

Memory

- Study slides of paintings with simple to complex compositions as the observation time increases from six seconds. Draw the paintings from memory in one minute, then in increasingly longer periods.   JH

Fluency

- Tell a story with quick sketches and see if your partner can read the story back to you, section by section.   E, JH
- Ellipses: Use flower pots as subjects and draw a series of discs centered around a common axis.   JH
- Develop a theme or a subject through several stages; the total work should be presented as a series, for example, a series of murals or a series of photographs.   JH
- Devote one small sketchbook to a changing part of your environment. Draw the object at specific time intervals over a period of weeks. Create a format for presenting the complete series at the completion of the project. (Weather conditions, plants, snow, a half-eaten piece of fruit are possible subjects.)   JH
- In six squares, rectangles, or circles change a realistic subject into an abstraction. Use Mondrian's *Flowering Tree* series as a model.   JH
- Take at least six photocopies of a self-portrait (drawing or photograph) and change each copy. The more variations, the better.   JH
- Draw a number of rectangles on a piece of canvas. Every three or four days make a quick oil sketch of cloud formations in one of the rectangles.   JH

Design Awareness

- The fractured image: Prepare a study of a face, an object, or an event. Then divide it into modules and reassemble them to create a fresh series of relationships. The viewer will be forced to mentally reorganize the format into its original state.   E, JH
- Group similar lines that reflect control of size, shade, and interval; then open and close the groups at intervals to achieve a warping effect on the surface of the page.   JH
- Working from negative spaces, draw a cluster of chairs.   JH

Three drawings from an Advanced Placement portfolio that demonstrate fluency. Matthew Chinian painted as he drew, spontaneously and directly.

Figure merges with ground as elements of both are fractured and placed in a complex system of light planes by the twelfth-grade artist.

An exercise to develop an understanding of form: bands of color were painted on cloth and arranged for study. This rendering is by a ninth-grade student.

- Draw the undulating surfaces of rippled paper, collapsed striped shirts, or unmade beds. The human face and torso can also be literally striped with tempera as subjects for drawing.   JH
- Psychological space: Use multiple perspectives of a subject in the same drawing for surrealistic effects.   JH
- Work on typographic layout or a calligraphic exercise.   JH
- Use a variety of textures as the main design component in a study.   E, JH
- Analyze the composition of complex paintings such as Picasso's *Guernica* and the historical subjects of Poussin, David, and Delacroix. Consider the use of shapes, line, tonal patterns, and other elements. First, try to do this verbally, then try to trace the elements using tracing paper. Concentrate on the directions and movements *beneath* the subject.   JH
- Design a still life using aspects of cubism such as open and close space through interpenetration of form and shifting planes.   JH
- Treat one subject in three different ways using color; for example, monochromatic, analogous, and complementary studies.   JH
- Demonstrate the use of color through the use of transparencies or transparency effects through media processes (for example, a light project).   JH

Boys will be boys: This fourth-grader's battle scene, incorporating action and costume, is one of a series of dozens of such drawings, each with its own story.

This painting of a Fourth of July parade by a senior high student (eleventh grade) has been reproduced in black and white half-tone so that the placement of shapes can be appreciated as abstract forms.

The gifted child may consciously select a difficult rather than a less demanding medium. This twelve-year-old preferred to work in wood rather than linoleum in the study of pubescent affection.

The strong, flowing quality of this print as it is placed upon a background of collage demonstrates the senior high school artist's awareness of the elements of design.

This senior high school student working in pen and ink and pencil applies his sensitivity to materials and knowledge of perspective to the study of domestic architecture.

Controls for Representational Art

- Training in the use of perspective: First make studies of small objects (piles of boxes on a table or the floor) and progress to large views (cityscapes).   JH
- Render basic geometric forms in different spatial positions.   JH
- Draw a pile of mannequins.   JH
- Vary the thickness of the line to achieve spatial illusions in drawing.   JH
- Extension of the square: Draw cards, bread slices, and books from varying angles.   JH

Problem Solving

- Each student received a bag full of odds and ends; everything in the bag must be used to create a piece of sculpture.   E, JH
- Design a game, toy, piece of furniture, garment, building, machine, or other object. The finished project may be the actual object, a model, or detailed drawings or plans.   E, JH
- Design housing for an alien from another planet that must be in constant motion as long as it is on the planet earth.   JH
- Attach a brush or a stick of compressed charcoal to the end of a broomstick or yardstick and draw from life as accurately as you can.   JH
- Pile the contents of a wastebasket on the floor. Rearrange the trash so that the custodian will think it is an artwork and will not disturb it.   JH
- Think of your days as divided into set time segments (for eating, sleeping, working, etc.) that cannot be changed. Create a pattern, design, or object based upon the fixed elements of time in your life.   JH

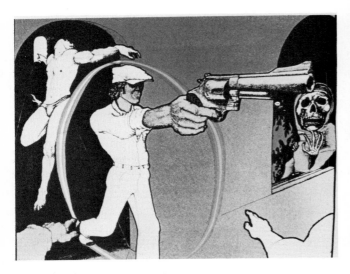

These two acrylic paintings by a boy from Texas show an interest in local subject matter and an ability to transfer the flat tones of Indian painting to a contemporary theme.

Problem-Solving in Art History
- Use the human figure to embody an attitude or to make a statement about the human condition.   E, JH
- Use drawings for social commentary.   E, JH
- Create a work with original subject matter in a historically documented style (primitive, medieval, cubistic, or expressionistic, for example). The work may be two- or three-dimensional.   JH
- Apply knowledge gained through a direct copy to a new situation.   JH

Feelings
- Explore automatic, spontaneous, unplanned drawing to express emotion (refer to the works of Max Ernst, Jackson Pollack, Robert Motherwell, and Arshile Gorki).   JH

Imagination
- Present subject matter in a new or greatly altered context or meaning. Create original storyboards for a TV commercial, a cartoon, or a film.   E, JH
- For the alteration of context: Create a landscape from a tree root or a sheet. People the landscape to give your drawing a new sense of scale.   E, JH

- Make drawings of private fantasies.   E, JH
- Make drawings of dreams, using surrealistic techniques.   JH
- Psychological space: Use multiple perspectives in rendering for surrealistic effects.   JH

Technique for Imaginative Ends

- Introduce collage techniques to extend the possibilities of an idea. Paste a number of sections of photographs on a large sheet of paper and then devise some way of connecting them through colors, ideas, and formal structure.   JH

Teaching the Artistically Gifted

One can only categorize up to a point. Art problems have a way of spilling over one area to another and their values often lie in the very fact that they deal with multiple problems at the same time. Categories are simply handles for one's thinking and can crack under stress.

Teaching the gifted requires teachers who can push their powers of invention beyond their accustomed range. The teacher who does not use her or his association with the gifted to extend her or his own capacity is missing out on a rare opportunity for personal growth.

Everything about an art program for the gifted can be stimulating, including the physical setting. The teacher should see that something in the room conveys the idea that business is not as usual. This can mean a display of new resource materials, original artwork that will be referred to during class, a new piece of equipment, new terms or artists' names, a listing or special assignments, or a special area for life drawing.

If a teacher can begin with a program that is rich in challenge, and then add to it the well-timed field trip, the occasional visiting artist, the resources that films, slides, books, and reproductions can offer, that teacher can, at the same time, create a model for what education in general should be. It is conceivable that this, by itself, could be the most valuable contribution that programs for the gifted can make.

This fourteen-year-old boy is developing an imaginary land-scape with surrealist overtones. Contour line is filled in with the flat tones of felt markers.

9 Location: Where Shall We Meet?

The answer to "Where shall we meet?" may seem obvious: the art room, of course. While this may be the first response, it is not necessarily the best solution. The location of a program can strongly influence what is learned. Consider each of the following locations, all of which have been used successfully.

The School

The school is a logical place to begin, especially if special classes are scheduled during school hours. If you plan the program for evenings or Saturday mornings, the budget may have to include custodial fees, and there may be problems in sharing someone else's space.

In a school art room you have total control. You can make your own rules, store your own supplies, use your own equipment, and structure your own environment.

Using a school art room need not limit the students to those who attend the school. Depending on the location and facilities, one school can serve gifted students throughout the community.

Schools without Walls

In the "school without walls" approach, the class has the whole community at its disposal: museums, art centers, art schools, colleges, artists' studios, industrial locations, parks, zoos, and other public and private facilities. Although it sounds promising, this approach entails extensive transportation logistics and is more appropriate for urban than rural areas. A "school without walls" also suggests a career rather than studio-oriented curriculum. But if you want to give your students a look at art and artists in the real world and are willing to work out scheduling and transportation, the school-at-large offers valuable exposure. Somewhere along the way, students should see where their training can ultimately lead them. The artists who use advanced technology or specialized conventional equipment (lathes, presses, foundries) can only be seen in their environments. In fact, every art program, for gifted and average students, could benefit from this experience at some point.

Centers in Higher Education

An art school or university art department can provide a professional atmosphere and role models in the form of college art majors. Art departments are also usually endowed with more space, better facilities, and a number of student works in progress.

Your class can also be of service to the institution in providing art education majors students they can work with. Department heads may also see your class as a source of recruitment for their own programs — so don't be shy about approaching them.

Museums

If an alliance with a museum can be made, the class has an opportunity to work with original artworks. (The term *museum* is used broadly here and includes any space designated to house artifacts that share some common frame of reference.) This may be the first time some students have ever visited a museum and the opportunity to relate curriculum to original art can add much to your program.

If the museum has studio area available to you, students can work with art materials as well as engage in appreciative activities. If a work area is not available, remember that sketch pads are portable and have been used for years in sketching from artwork. There is also a longstanding European tradition of students painting in galleries, although this may take some persuading on your part in North American museums.

Artists' Studios

In some programs, individuals and small groups have worked directly with artists in their own studios. This apprentice approach is particularly appropriate for a select group of limited enrollment. In any case, most artists are happy to host at least one meeting a year of any group of students they feel are truly interested. If a dozen such invitations can be obtained, a teacher has the makings of a unique program with not one, but many teachers. Send out twenty requests and a dozen artists are likely to respond favorably.

Churches and Other Locations

Churches and synagogues have also donated space to special art classes, as have recreation departments, factories, and grange halls. Be prepared for restrictions, however, particularly if the space is shared by others. There may be restrictions on time and equipment, regulations on clean-up, and other conditions.

In most cases, though, you can expect to pay only for custodial costs and insurance — a bargain.

10 Evaluation: How Far Have We Come?

Evaluation is an accepted fact of life in American education. Parents, teachers, and administrators — everyone with a stake in the schooling process — want to know not only what is happening, but if programs are worth the time, expense, and effort entailed. It should also be borne in mind that the information gained from an evaluation can be used not only to justify a program, but to help state the case for continuing or expanding it. Used for diagnostic purposes, a good evaluation can also indicate weaknesses that may need rethinking.

During the evaluative phase, accurate information must be assembled and useful conclusions drawn from the data gathered. There are, of course, many ways to evaluate a program, but whatever method is chosen it usually begins with the program's stated goal. If a program's goal is to "help children to become more curious about art," then we will want to know if any of the students are indeed more curious about the subject at the program's conclusion.

What is the best way to get such information? Examinations? Student interviews? In just what ways would the students show increased curiosity about art? Perhaps the "development of curiosity" is an unrealistic goal, or perhaps the goal has merit, but there is no reliable way of studying its existence. If, instead, the goal is to "ensure a basic knowledge of major artists and art movements since World War II," then evaluation becomes more manageable since it is easy to devise an examination to test knowledge. These are the kinds of considerations that confront evaluators.

The Evaluator

The selection of the evaluator is important if only because of the expense that this may involve. *Inside* evaluators, that is, personnel from the local administration, are the least expensive since their salaries are already accounted for. The amount of time that an evaluator can give to a project must be taken into consideration and costs for typing and duplication of reports must be budgeted, although such expenses are often absorbed by the system. *Outside* evaluators, often professionals who specialize in this field, can be objective in a way that may be denied someone who is known to the local staff. In either case, evaluators should hold the respect of the teachers and possess professional credentials.

The system of evaluation that is to be used should be made known in advance. It is worth the few professional meetings required for the evaluator to explain the methods to be used, to elicit suggestions, and, above all, to enlist the staff as partners in the task. Orientation sessions are also important in establishing the terms to be used. This should be done in the early stages of the program rather than at the conclusion.

Types of Evaluations

Several terms are commonly used in describing types of program evaluations. Here are some brief definitions.

Summative evaluation An evaluation of a program after its conclusion.

Formative evaluation A continuing assessment of a program in progress.

Responsive evaluation is also a study of the ongoing life of a program, but it does not necessarily measure results against stated goals. Instead, it notes changes, gathers data, questions the students, teachers, and parents concerned with the program, and seeks out issues that may not have existed when the program was instituted. A responsive evaluation assumes that goals can change and may not have been worth making in the first place, and that other, possibly more important, factors should be noted. At some point, all the data (photographs, charts, interviews, films, etc.) are gathered into a portrayal or exhibit to which both the school and the public are invited.

Preordinate evaluation An evaluation that relates only to the stated goals of a program. Achievement and performance tests and observation checklists are the most common forms of this type of evaluation.

Since most programs for the gifted require special funding, for which careful accountability is demanded, preordinate assessments are usually favored over responsive evaluations. However, a well-rounded composite assessment should incorporate elements of both types of evaluation. Concluding a program with an imaginative portrayal using an array of media from video to original works

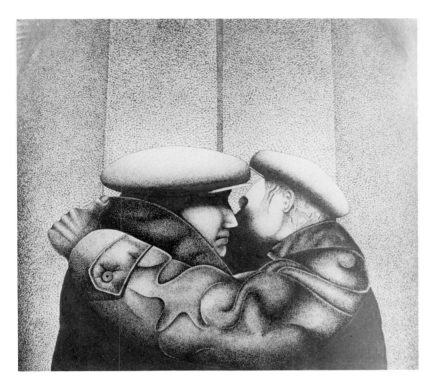

A strong emotional element is captured in this meticulously textured drawing of an embrace. A freer, bolder approach focuses upon a pair of hands to evoke an emotional response in the viewer. Both artists were in senior high school.

This ten-year-old has already had a one-man exhibition. His work is characterized by great variety of subject and high imaginative content. The teacher obviously provides the support required by all talented children.

of art is certainly effective, especially if the exhibit is followed by a group discussion that solicits questions, reactions, and suggestions for improvement from the viewers.

Evaluation of Student Work

Since the evaluation of a program's effectiveness can only be based on an evaluation of student performance, it is especially important to keep regular records of the students. One way to do this is through an **anecdotal record**. In this ongoing evaluation, periodic notations are made by the teacher of significant student behavior.

The following chart presents one way of keeping an anecdotal record. The first three columns allow the activity to be recorded. The criteria section lists specific standards that are to be met. The criteria reflect stated objectives and so may vary from project to project. In the last section the teacher can note the quality of the work as *exemplary*, *acceptable*, or *low*. Exemplary work would be above the student's normal production. Acceptable refers to the large body of adequate work; work judged as low reflects both lack of effort and understanding, or some factor of incapacity, such as color blindness.

Many other methods exist for evaluating what students gain from a special program. Here are some standard methods that can be used alone or in combination.

Portfolio Examination (ongoing or summative)
Through portfolio examination the teacher can chart the development of each student's work. The clearer the focus of the curriculum, the easier this is to do. For example, a drawing portfolio

ANECDOTAL WORK RECORD OF _____

Subject	Media	Class Sessions	CRITERIA SECTION			JUDGMENT		
			Sensitivity To Media	Ability to Capture Likeness	Proportion	Exemplary	Acceptable	Low
Realistic Portrait Head	Clay	Four	Sally's surfaces are not over-worked and are richly textured. Shows influence of Jacob Epstein	Easily recogniz-able	Structure of skull bears poor relation to surface		X	
Imaginative Portrait	Clay	One	Sally's feeling for clay really produced some exciting results. The imaginative element seemed to free her. Worked very quickly at first, then hit a plateau and fin-ished with great care.	Not an issue	Conscious-ly distorted natural propor-tions to achieve her intent	X		

may reveal more about a student's development than one that in-cludes photography, sculpture, painting, and drawing, all used to explore different concepts. However, if the program's goal was to develop curiosity through investigation, such a wide range of media could be appropriate. The goal could also have been explored through in-depth work in one medium.

This category can also include assessment of non-studio projects, such as written reports on artists and artistic movements.

Time Study (ongoing or summative)
This is a record of the amount of attention a student devotes to a par-ticular problem.

Direct Experience (summative)
Specific tasks are assigned at a program's end to determine if the students' skills have improved through participation in the program.

Objective Tests (summative)
A multiple choice, true/false, or sentence completion test can be given to ascertain the degree of information retained by the students on material covered in the program (art careers, new vocabulary, the names of artists and art movements, techniques, whatever was taught).

Inventoried Experience (summative)
Students can be asked to keep a journal of drawings, personal observations, poetry, pieces for a collage, etc. This can be very revealing if the student is assured the material is confidential.

They can also list various self-initiated results of the program: the art books they read on their own, the museums they visited without adult suggestion, the new artists, techniques, or personal goals they discovered in the program.

A parent questionnaire can help verify these results. A parent can state whether the student returned to a museum on his or her own; discussed the class activities at home; purchased or borrowed art reproductions and books from the library.

A year or two after the program students may complete another questionnaire which would allow the staff to evaluate the long term effects of the program.

Student Evaluation

The perceptions and feelings of students often differ from those of teachers. Assessing pupil reaction is vital for the simple reason that no program can exist without the support of its participants. Since special art programs are seldom, if ever, required, teachers and planners must plan an agenda that is both challenging and pleasurable. If students feel a program is not succeeding, they will usually stop coming to class rather than discuss the problem with the teacher. One way to find out how things stand is to devise reaction questionnaires to be given during the course of the program as well as at its conclusion.

Typical Questioning Styles

A teacher can create any style of questionnaire he or she is comfortable with. Here are three common types.

Checking response (for feelings and attitudes)
From the list below, check the statement that best describes your general reaction to this course.

_____ I am satisfied with the way things are going.
_____ I am not satisfied with the course.
_____ I am not satisfied with the course because of what I am asked to do.
_____ I am not satisfied with the course because of my teacher.
_____ I am not satisfied with the course because _____.
_____ I would like to continue the course next semester.
_____ I like the course, but feel it can be improved in the following ways:

Completion response (for factual information)
One artist I have come to like through this course is _____.
I have improved my work in the following ways: _____.

Matching response (1 to 5 scale)
I think the class should be asked to do more work outside class.
5 strongly agree
4 agree
3 agree slightly
2 disagree
1 strongly disagree

Other statements that lend themselves to a 1 to 5 range of reactions:

The class should go on more field trips to museums and art galleries.
I feel the teacher could make me work harder in this program.

Such questions can also be used in personal interviews. Although interviews consume more time, they do encourage students to share and to expand upon their ideas. The taped interview, however, is more difficult to assess in an objective way because the student may ramble on in an attempt to clarify his/her thinking.

The danger in creating questionnaires is the temptation to ask "safe" questions; that is, to present choices in such a way as to reflect positively upon the program. For example:

Please check one of the following:

_____ I feel that this program is very good, but can still be improved.
_____ Has given me more than I expected.
_____ Is what we should be doing in the regular art program.
_____ Is a wonderful idea and should be continued.

Obviously, none of the above responses is going to make anyone appear in a negative light. Since a questionnaire must be objective and fair to all parties, two or more teachers should share the task of preparation with at least one disinterested party who has no personal stake in the success or failure of the program.

Evaluation Model

"The Museum is People" was a Saturday morning (10 A.M. to 12 noon) class initiated by the author as a joint effort between a suburban school system and a major urban museum. A self-selection identification procedure was used and the program was open to the first twenty secondary students who applied. Its goal was to introduce students to museums and to new ways of looking at art. In the announcement that went to each junior and senior high school it was stated that participants would be expected to:

- arrive at the museum on time using their own means of transportation.
- be prepared to study artworks through discussion and studio activities.
- keep a sketchbook.
- prepare a special project if the participant was a senior high school student desiring credit.

The funding of the program was shared by the students, who paid a nominal tuition ($1.50 a session), and the budget of the art department. The major expenses involved were the salary of the teacher and sketchbooks purchased for each class member. The teacher was a museum docent, selected not only because of expertise in art history and skill in teaching, but because her affiliation with the museum assured access to areas denied the general public. The program was designed to be held at the museum for twenty sessions (based upon the time required to earn a high school credit). The objectives of the program were:

- To instill positive attitudes toward museums
- To view the study of art through intense observation and serious discussion as a legitimate activity
- To convey new information about museums, particularly in the area of operations and careers
- To convey new information about art history through the study of selected artworks
- To create an awareness of the difference between reproductions of art and art in its original state
- To create some personal momentum so that the student, in some way, continued the study of art on his or her own.

The sessions were based on the following topics:

1. Defining a museum
2. The museum as a cataloger and collector
3. The museum as preserver
4. The museum as restorer
5. The museum as exhibitor
6. The museum as educator
7. The museum as performer and image-maker
8. The museum and security
9. The museum's facilities for feeding and providing such things as sitting areas, resting areas, and washrooms, and clear directions for all the different ages and types of people who visit
10. The museum as archeologist

The remaining sessions were spent in the galleries studying the works on display. These sessions progressed from general, broad topics to subjects with a limited focus, e.g., broad topic — the French Impressionist Collection; limited focus — one painting, such as Vincent van Gogh's *Ravine*.

If the group spent an entire session on one painting or artist it was in no way a hindrance; indeed, it encouraged the group to probe with greater depth into the meaning of the work.

The evaluation consisted mostly of responsive techniques. During the sessions, the evaluator visited the classes to get a sense of the learning climate. And at the end of the program, student projects and photographs of the class in action were exhibited for art teachers, administrators and parents. The purpose of the exhibit was to explain the nature and purpose of the program. At the end of the program, the evaluator also used the following techniques:

- Commented on student sketchbooks
- Studied projects informally, avoiding critical assessment
- Displayed the students' comparative studies of several art works and their analytical studies of a particular style or artist
- Displayed the students' reports which contained their personal observations and responses to an artist's life and work
- Made note of attendance records
- Distributed questionnaires to the students to determine how they felt the program could be improved and if they would continue the class next year (In this particular program, 90% of the students voted positively.)

Conclusion

When all is said and done, the two most direct ways to determine the success or failure of a program are the attendance records and the desire of students to continue their involvement. If the students stop coming, if they have no desire to continue, and if there is no evidence on their part of wanting to pursue museum- and art-related activities on their own, we can assume that the program is in trouble, or has failed. As a successful theatrical producer once noted, "The box office never lies!"

11 Dissemination: Letting People Know

Upon the completion of the program, the task of dissemination should be considered. The reasons for this are practical: future funding may rest upon the accuracy and thoroughness of a final report, or it may simply be sound public relations policy to let the public know about the good work being carried on in its school system.

Final reports usually take two forms: The formal report provides a full record of factual information, including identification, curriculum, location, attendance figures, and evaluation. Its function is to describe, not praise. The informal report is also descriptive, but in other ways. It may be anecdotal in nature, and may contain statements by students, teachers, and parents (nearly always of a complimentary nature). If the publication budget allows, an informal report may also use photographs, a professionally planned layout, and quality stock paper. Since many people will want copies of this information, someone must also be prepared to handle packaging, mailing, and postage. Some programs charge a fee for their reports; others allot a certain number for free distribution.

The formal report is likely to be a necessity; everything beyond this will rest upon the personal energies of the director of the program. Information sheets should be prepared for newspaper publicity at the beginning and at the end of the program. If there are any highlights in the program, such as visiting artists or special events, releases should be sent to local newspapers as events occur.

Other forms of dissemination include:

- A proposal to state and national conferences to present an overview of the program through slides or films.
- An article written for such magazines such as *School Arts, Arts and Activities,* and *Gifted Child Quarterly.*
- An evening presentation for parents when slides, films, and projects are all complete. This can be combined with an open house on the last day of the program. In addition to explaining exhibits, students can run workshops for parents in the activities carried on in the program.
- A traveling exhibition can be assembled and sent to schools, conferences, and community centers such as libraries, the central administration office, city hall, and other facilities.

The dynamic treatment of forms surrounding the subject takes this study of a horse out of the realm of the commonplace. The artist was in the tenth grade.

- Directors should also be alerted to any publications that gather together models of programs, and attempt to have a description of their own programs included.
- Those who can speak for the program should make themselves available to community groups, (Kiwanis, art clubs, PTAs) to present a slide lecture. Nothing has greater impact than a visual review of children creating art and working with teachers, then showing the end results.
- In the case of programs lasting a year or more, a periodic newsletter to parents can inform them of current activities.

Student work should be included whenever possible. There are now inexpensive ways of reproducing a collection of student work. For instance:

- Portfolios of work are less expensive than bound editions.
- Prints and drawings can be published rather than photos of crafts, sculpture or paintings.
- Drawings and/or prints can be photocopied
- Large editions of prints can be run.

The dissemination process implies that you are proud of your work and you want people to know about it, and when people are informed, it is easier to persuade them to support you for the following stage of development. Also, since it was their money that got things going in the first place, they may feel they have a right to know the results of the program.

Model Programs

Part Three

A seven-year-old child in a special program works on a large (16" x 24") woodcut, an activity that would not normally be offered in a regular school program.

12 Examples of Programs

The number of programs for the gifted has been increasing nationwide in the past decade, mostly at the senior high level. On this level the most impressive development has been in the thirty-five to forty (the number keeps growing each year) special high schools for the visual and performing arts.

In this section, examples of several kinds of programs are reviewed to give the reader some idea of how the issues discussed in the previous sections have been approached, if not always solved. Each program was selected to represent a full range of efforts, from the school to state levels; from nonfunded to well-endowed. The italicized portions in a program direct attention to its unique features.

The School Level

Pull-Out or Released Time Program
Bigelow Junior High School, Newton, Massachusetts

Level   Junior high school, ninth grade

Initiators   Two staff art teachers

Funding   No special funding required

Identification   The teachers selected the students based on the quality of their work, their work habits and attitudes (persistence and concentration), and their status in non-art subjects. Twelve students were studied for five weeks before they were accepted in the program.

Objectives   To develop the relationships between drawing skill and the powers of imagination
To provide career information by relating topics of study to selected artists
To give group discussion a more important part in the learning process

Structure   The art teachers worked with the principal to clear two hours a week for the group for one semester. The non-art faculty were then asked to release the students involved from their classes twice a week. Once the teachers were persuaded of the merit of the idea, scheduling problems were eliminated. Students were simply excused to

A mixed group of parents and children join together in a drawing of wall sized proportion. This is one method of sustaining parents' interest in their children's talents.

come to the art room at a designated time. The art teachers conducted the class as a team.

Curriculum The content of the program fell into two categories: drawing and Oriental art. The intensive drawing sessions used imaginative work based upon Surrealist ideas, and dealt with problems of representation. The second phase, Oriental art, was a special interest of one of the teams. It centered on history, calligraphy and brush techniques.

Evaluation Student evaluation forms were used, and the results were positive. The art supervisor also displayed the work of the class at the central exhibition area. Upon the request of the class, the art teachers sent the students' names to the high school art department heads so that the students could continue to work in an advanced group.

Contact Joanna Meyler or Sue Kwasnick
Bigelow Junior High School
42 Vernon Street
Newton, MA 02158

Self-Help Program within a District

Self-Study Units for the Gifted in Art
Worcester, Massachusetts

Level   Upper Elementary

Initiators   Elementary art staff

Funding $1,100 from the Commonwealth In-Service Institute, an organization concerned with the improvement of classroom instruction. This amount covered nominal fees for consultants and teachers, and costs of materials. Other materials came from recycling centers and donations. Teachers donated much of their time.

Identification   Consultants spoke to teachers at biweekly meetings on research, methods of identification, model programs, and the characteristics of artistically gifted children. Participants were selected upon recommendation from the classroom teacher, art teacher, and peers. Forty-four schools were involved from which 350 students were selected.

Goal   To provide an art program for gifted students without removing them from their regular classes.

Structure   Since the target group remained in the regular classes, no additional formal structure was necessary. Students worked on this after they completed their normal work load. The program ran for a full school year.

Curriculum   The curriculum consisted of five packaged instructional units designed for individualized learning. The units, prepared by teachers during a series of workshops, consisted of suggested activities beyond the regular curriculum. Each unit covered a different topic and the nature of the units varied with the subject. The units were borrowed on a rotating basis, through the art director's office.

The ceramics unit, for example, was organized in three boxes. It included tools used by professional ceramicists, vocabulary lists, self-study guides with questions, slides and reproductions on the history of ceramics, and clay activities related to the slides.

The development of the units also brought about an in-service phase, as teachers had to update their knowledge of unit topics and their corresponding techniques.

Evaluation Classroom teachers, art teachers and administrators held informal discussions at the end of the year. The reaction was favorable and the program was scheduled to be repeated, but the new tax structure in Massachusetts eliminated the funding.

Contact Marilyn Goodman
Associate Director of Studio Programs
Clark University School at Worcester Art Museum
55 Salisbury Street
Worcester, MA 01608

The District Level

Gifted and Talented in the Senior High School
Frederick, Maryland

Level Junior and senior high school

Initiator Evolved out of discussions suggested by Federal Projects Coordinator

Funding A Title IV grant provided the initial funds for the instructor, art materials, custodial time, guest speakers, and other expenses. When grant monies were exhausted, the school system took over the funding. This program has been running for five years now.

Identification Identification was based on teacher nomination, student application, creativity, and artistic characteristics instruments.

Goal To extend services through a special setting. To promote growth through working with peers.

Structure Classes were held in the evening to avoid conflicts in daytime schedules. A studio course was offered, supplemented by slide lectures, at least two hours of studio work, weekly critique sessions, and field trips to museums in Baltimore and Washington, D.C. The instructor who was used throughout the program was selected because he was a practicing artist as well as an outstanding art teacher. He was joined by invited guest specialists for particular classes.

Curriculum A major theme, such as "Man and Environment: The Figure in Space," was selected as the basis for all activities. Different themes were selected for each year. Before the students began working on a large sculptured piece, they studied the work of artists such as Bacon and Matisse in relation to the visualization of the human figure in a variety of media. The course was climaxed by the mounting of one student's seven-foot concrete sculpture at the entrance of the city park. The work was selected by the mayor and a committee of qualified judges. Although the work is abstract, it has been accepted by the community.

Evaluation   Students were tested before and after the program to assess drawing skill and information about art (processes, personalities, terminology, etc.).

Contact   Carol Kehne
Curriculum Specialist in Art Education
115 E. Church Street
Frederick, Maryland 21701

An Informal Club Program in a Small City

Gifted and Talented Kids and the Visual Arts
Pittsfield, Massachusets

Level   Elementary

Initiator   Art director

Funding   Local school district: use of regularly scheduled teacher time

Identification   The art director distributed a packet of identification materials (characteristics, checklists, and tests) to the art staff and to all sixth grade teachers. This material was gathered from her own study of six other programs. The teachers were asked to study the information and to use their own judgment in selecting two sixth graders from each participating school. As the program developed, lower grades were included, on the assumption that the older children would assist in teaching second graders. All applicants were personally interviewed by the art director, and a certain percentage of students were admitted for therapeutic reasons rather than for performance in art. Eight students comprised the group, all above the second grade. This was the average for the ten schools.

Lois, at the ages of seven and eight, has created a world through her drawings, populated almost entirely by horses. Lois draws many kinds of horses in innumerable positions. Her horses have saddles and riders, pull carriages and explode from starting gates, but most remarkably, they sit at desks, carry umbrellas, plant vegetables, and mind their mothers.

Goal Goals were never discussed as such in the director's report, although some conclusion can be drawn from summary comments. If, in the director's view, an "open-ended accepting atmosphere" was to be created through "special attention" given by "enthusiastic and intelligent leaders," then we can assume that this was the goal.

Structure An art club was established that met every Wednesday afternoon from October through June. This was a pull-out approach since the students had to miss other classes at that time. As in all such situations, someone had to convince the classroom teacher that this was not lost time.

The art teacher assigned to the school was scheduled so as to have two periods free one afternoon a week. There was, however, strong administrative support from the principal who was involved in a systemwide planning of services for the gifted, at the request of the superintendent. The project began small, with two sixth-grade students from each school. More students were added as they were identified.

Curriculum This was a free-choice program. One child worked in papier-mâché, another in ceramics; one preferred drawing for fantasy, while another drew nonobjective geometric shapes. Toward the end of the program, the director introduced a formal lesson in color that required personal research. The students objected to this shift in style midstream and were quick to voice their opinion. Another idea that did not work as planned was the assumption that older children would welcome the chance to work with second-graders. The older ones were not only reluctant to participate in this service, but resented the presence of seven-year-olds (who were eventually dropped from the program). As the program developed, other ideas were incorporated, such as the following:

- Students were permitted to work at the two high schools with both staff and students. (It is interesting to note that the high school students did not share the sixth-graders' reluctance to work with those younger than themselves.)
- Field trips to the local library and museum.

Evaluation   Questionnaires were sent out to parents, teachers and children twice during the year. Reactions were collated into chart form, from which the following is taken:

Teacher reaction   "Opportunity for social involvement was valuable for a gifted student who was under-developed socially." "Students in art club should share with class."

Parent reaction   "We are delighted and encouraged by this enrichment of Beth's life." To another parent the best feature was the child's "opportunity to choose an art project for herself and then have the time for satisfying completion."

Children's reactions   One child appreciated being able to "work on whatever we wanted...for a long time." Another said, "Kids were always asking , how do you get in?"

On balance, all forms of assessment led to the following suggestions for the future:

- Ideally, a gifted program should begin at lower levels and continue with the same population until the end of elementary school.
- Selection and identification should be more accurate.
- Classroom teachers should be involved to a greater extent at all stages of program development.
- Some system should be created to ensure that students make up work missed in art and academic classes.
- The curriculum should begin in a more structured style and then move toward increased freedom and responsibility.

Contact   Winfred Bell, Barbara Kulpinsky, or Jeanne Walsh
Dawes School
Pittsfield Public Schools
Pittsfield, MA 01201

An Interdisciplinary Approach for a City System

Aesthetic Education for the Intellectually Gifted Child
William Ward School, New Rochelle, New York

Level Elementary, fifth and sixth grades

Initiators Member of administration staff

Funding Funded by Special Education Director of Board of Education with grant money from state and local sources.

Identification Children were selected from top level of IOWA Verbal and Mathematical abilities tests. General academic achievement level as attested by teachers and principal, using the rating system of the New York State Guidelines for identification of the gifted and talented. Applicants had to show competence in at least two out of seven areas in both art and academic subjects.

Objectives The purposes of the program were stated in poetic terms: "to develop courage," "the impulse to risk new, difficult, roads less traveled," "to build group esprit," "to develop a sense of trust," and "to develop a sense of identity." In more conventional terms, the planners wanted to develop risk taking, to provide greater intellectual challenge, and to help children regard themselves in more revealing ways. These aims were to be accomplished through *interdisciplinary* means using visual experience as but one part of the total experience.

Structure A pull-out approach was used in which students were excused from the classroom. An art teacher, a media expert and a drama and movement teacher worked as a team. Weekly planning sessions were programmed into the schedule to pool impressions of students. The length of the program was one year.

Curriculum *Phase 1* Children developed characters that embodied some personal fantasy of wish fulfillment and developed their new persona through painting, mime, improvisation, and the creating of narratives, using appropriate language and dialogue. Characters were painted and posted on classroom walls. Dialogue was tape recorded and performed in dramatic scenes.
Phase 2 A study of Shakespeare's *Julius Caesar* which focused upon the development and interaction of characters. It also included the

study of Latin, of Roman culture, and of the structure of Roman society. During this phase, each child took on the identity of a Roman citizen and researched the life-style of his subject.

The culminating activity was a Roman banquet followed by short plays in Latin. Appropriate decorations and architectural settings had been created for the event.

Evaluation The Director of Special Education invited several consultants to observe, analyze and assess. Each one wrote narrative, evaluative descriptions. Parents were in attendance and made informal evaluations. Evaluations were consistently positive.

Contact Ellen Handler Spitz
37 Iselin Terrace
Larchmont, N.Y. 10538

A Township Works with a Museum

Art Enrichment and Sculpture Program
Washington Township, Indianapolis, Indiana, and the Indianapolis Museum of Art

Level Elementary, fifth and sixth grades

Initiators A self-appointed committee of twelve elementary art teachers evolved the plan and presented it at a principals' meeting for their support.

Funding Shared by all participating schools. The amount was minimal: $50 from each school, the source of money determined by each school. Pursuing grant sources was abandoned because of scheduling deadlines or because the potential funding organization did not support the idea. Some materials were purchased, some donated by the schools.

Identification The following criteria were used:

- The Renzuli-Hartman scale
- Learning and motivational assessment by classroom teachers
- Creative and artistic potential as assessed by art teachers
- Special creativity measures developed by a team of art teachers

Sixty students were selected, five from each of the twelve schools involved.

Objectives　The initiating committee hoped this program would enable students to:

1. Define sculpture and related terms.
2. Explain how sculpture is created.
3. Demonstrate use of sculptural tools, materials, and techniques.
4. Create a sculpture.
5. Describe how cultural aspects influence sculpture.
6. Analyze the relationship of sculpture to the environment.
7. Describe ways that sculpture can enrich our lives.
8. Critique the completed sculptural projects.
9. Evaluate sculpture as a personally satisfying art form.

Structure　The program had three bases of operation: two schools on either side of the city and the museum. The children met six times during the school year, four times during the school day and twice after school. When in school, the classes worked in three-dimensional techniques; when in the museum, in appreciative activities.

　　The children were divided into five groups. The museum determined the number of groups based on the docents who were available. Upon arrival, each child was assigned a color-coded, shaped name tag. The name tags were worn each session at the museum. The docents and art teachers were similarly identified. Since there were five groups and five students from each school, it was a simple matter to mix students from the various schools. Since the children did not know the others in their group, they were forced to make new friends.

Curriculum　The curriculum was based on the objectives listed above and included input from museum personnel and local artists. All activities included the observation and study of sculpture as well as hands-on work. The work involved drawings and three-dimensional studies based on sculpture in the museum. Students selected their own materials; some preferred to model, others chose to carve or make constructions.

　　At the final session all students were asked to display their work and to study the entire exhibit. Parents, administrators, staff, IMA staff, docents, and four visiting artists were invited to participate in a final critique. This took place in a school gymnasium, where tables were set up. Each table grouping consisted of six students (with their displayed work), a discussion leader (art teacher), and parents. A small side room off the cafeteria was used for showing slides taken at all the sessions (at IMA and at the schools). Pictures taken by the art staff, the school's A-V office, and newspapers during all the activities were labeled and displayed so that the children could enjoy a review of all the public relations efforts. A certificate was presented to each participating student.

Evaluation   Evaluation forms were given to the twelve art teachers to distribute to the students and another form was sent to each child's home to be completed by the child with his or her parent. The classroom teacher and the art teacher completed forms designed to obtain input. The IMA also included its evaluation form. Evaluations indicated that more studio time needed to be built into the program, that the program should be continued the following year, and that additional grade levels should be included.

The program is now in its second year and is considered a success.

Contact   Norma Bennett
Harcourt Elementary School
M.S.D. Washington Township
Indianapolis, IN 46240

A City Works with a Museum

Milwaukee's Art Center Satellite Program
Milwaukee Art Center

Level   Senior high school, eleventh and twelfth grades

Initiators   Director of Art, Milwaukee Public Schools and Curator of Education, Milwaukee Art Center

Funding   The Milwaukee School System with facilities supplied by the Art Center

Identification   Self-identification is used. Students requesting admission have to have taken one art course at their high school. Admission is on a first come, first served basis, but students do not remain unless they can meet the demands of the program. The staff engages in active recruiting by taking a specially prepared slide tape to schools. Thirty students were accommodated each semester.

Objectives   The objectives are varied:

- To facilitate U.S. District Court order for desegregation
- To promote cultural and historical appreciation and understanding through use of Art Center facilities
- To develop artistic and creative expression of students
- To familiarize students with other art institutions in the area of the Arts Center

Structure   The program takes one school semester with daily two hour class periods five days a week. But transportation is provided for outlying districts.

One high school credit unit in art is awarded if specific assignments are fulfilled.

Curriculum   In studio activities work is evaluated in terms of ability to solve a given problem and to develop an individual style. Appreciative and critical activities included working with specialists in the museum and assisting them in mounting exhibitions and other curatorial functions.

The curriculum is divided into long and short units with occasional connections made between two segments. For example, a unit on architecture might be related to one that deals with the nature of the Art Center which is considered to be an important example of local contemporary architecture.

At the end of the program, the students mount an exhibition of their work at the Art Center, for which they design and distribute posters, and plan and conduct the opening reception.

Evaluation   Written tests based upon slides of the artwork studied are used to evaluate what students have learned (e.g., showing two slides of architecture simultaneously and asking the students to point out similarities and differences between the architectural styles). Follow-up reports are submitted by alumni who have had time to consider the program with greater perspective.

Contact   Carolyn White
Milwaukee Art Center
750 N. Lincoln Memorial Drive
Milwaukee, WI 53202

A Consortium Pattern for Museum Collaboration

Project Art Band
Lincoln, Massachusetts

Level Middle school, sixth, seventh, and eighth grades

Initiators Four neighboring school systems joined with a museum (The De-Cordova Museum, Lincoln, Massachusetts) to plan a grant from the ESEA (Elementary and Secondary Educational Act) Title IV-C program for gifted children.

Funding A three-year grant of $155,000 was awarded by ESEA.

Identification One hundred children were admitted from among 2,500 sixth, seventh, and eighth graders. Project Art Band employed multifaceted methods of identification:

- Subjective assessment of student abilities from teachers, peers, and parents.
- The Torrance Test of Creative Thinking (to satisfy an ESEA Title IV-C requirement).
- Two instruments to assess skills in visual operations: a visual narrative instrument, which asked the children to tell a story with pictures, and a visual memory instrument, which asked applicants to draw a Van Gogh painting from memory after viewing the work. This test revealed powers of recall, a significant factor in visually gifted children, and indicated their ability to transpose one form of art into another. Graders were trained to score the exercises. This was a complicated procedure since the narrative test had eighteen items to score and the memory instrument had seventeen points to assess. (See the Appendix.)

The sum of all test scores, the directors reasoned, would produce a reasonably reliable profile of a child with visual and creative aptitude. Those who scored in the top five percent of the total profile were admitted to the program.

Objectives Project Art Band is an ambitious project. For students its objectives are:

- To identify visually talented students

- To improve the self concept of visually talented students
- To improve attitude of visually talented students toward school and the arts
- To expand students' skill in, interest in, and knowledge of the arts
- To continually monitor the project's effectiveness and make ongoing changes

Teacher education is a major element of the program, as these objectives and activities show:

- To increase teachers' and mentors' awareness of and attitude toward visually talented students, their strengths, and their problems
  Activity 1 Seminars on gifted and talented students (psychology of, strategies of instruction, socialization, etc.)
  Activity 2 Ongoing meetings to address problems in working with visually talented students
- To provide technical assistance to the local school districts and to teachers in the implementation of programs for visually talented students
  Activity 1 Seminars, skill courses, and problem-solving meetings with administrators and teachers
  Activity 2 Organization, implementation, and evaluation of the program
- To improve teachers' skills in the visual arts
  Activity Participation in DeCordova Museum School classes

A conference in the early stages of the program involved several major figures in art education and was on the level of any national conference of an educational nature. The ongoing use of consultants with impressive professional credentials was consistent with Project Art Band's concern for quality in all critical points of decision making.

Structure The students were allowed to leave their schools five times a month to visit art centers and also to serve as apprentices to local artists. The schools also rearranged schedules in order to allow for the formation of special weekly classes for participants. The staff of the DeCordova Museum, in turn, developed their own series of weekly

A delicate balance is maintained between pencil and light washes of watercolor in this still life by a senior high student.

classes and presented a spring exhibition of student work, carried out at both the museum and the schools.

Curriculum The classes engaged in such activities as drawing (narrative, observation, and memory), painting, photography, stained glass, illustrations, intensive discussions with mentors, discussions about works exhibited at the art center, and field trips selected for specific content-related goals.

Evaluation The evaluation included two examinations — one given before the program and one at the conclusion. In this way, the degrees of change in attitudes and information about art could be assessed. There was the Piers-Harris Self-Concept Scale and the National Assessment of Art Tests. The project staff who assumed control of the evaluation modes employed anecdotal journals of students and their activities, and periodic inquiries of a less formal nature with parents, teachers, and administrators. The mentors (artists who worked with students) carried out their own assessments. Classroom teachers were personally interviewed to determine their awareness of and attitudes toward visually talented students. Newsletters from the museum as well as distribution of the evaluation report kept everyone concerned in touch with the progress of the program.

Contact David Baker
Department of Art and Art Education
Louisiana State University
Baton Rouge, LA 70816

Extensive Multiple Funding for a State Program

Oklahoma Summer Arts Institute
Quartz Mountain State Park, Lone Wolf, Oklahoma

Initiators   A group of parents appealed to the Oklahoma State Arts Council for a program for children gifted in all of the arts. The Council then appointed a planning committee of cultural and educational leaders. The Institute currently operates under a board of directors.

Funding   Perhaps the most complex and far-reaching of any program studied. Private foundation grants (matching grants from the Kerr Foundation), corporate grants (Phillips Petroleum), scholarship contribuitons from civic and arts organizations, federal and state grants (including a donation from the Oklahoma Department of Tourism and Recreation), and memberships. Student tuition is $400, which covers one-third of the cost. Contributions are listed under the following headings: benefactors are listed under the following headings: benefactors, underwriters, patrons, sponsors, supporting members, "in-kind services," and memorial funds.

Identification   Two years of high school art courses are required for painting and printmaking; submission of a portfolio containing six original works is also required.

For photography, darkroom experience is required. The portfolio must include six 8" x 10" original black and white prints processed by the student.

Any student who is selected can attend. If a student cannot afford the tuition, it is the job of the director to raise the money. Two hundred are accepted each summer.

Goal   To provide an intermediate step between public school programs and career decisions by offering students intensive work with professionals of both national and state reputation, such as Fritz Scholder in painting and Maria Tallchief in dance.

Structure   Sessions run for two weeks. Morning classes are in the student's area of specialization. Films and special events are scheduled in the early afternoon; a class in the student's chosen area is scheduled later in the afternoon. Electives are taken in the evening.

Curriculum	Three subject areas are offered (painting, printmaking, and photography), with an intense professional focus.
	Electives in other arts areas (dance and drama) are required in evening classes.
	"Conversations with Artists" are held for all students, and guest artists visit for two- or three-day residences in all arts areas.
	Performances are offered by students as well as faculty and visiting artists.
Evaluation	Students fill out a form that deals with reactions and general impressions of staffing and administration, programming, and weekend performances.
Contact	Mary Y. Frates, Director OSAI Room 640 Jim Thorpe Building Oklahoma City, OK 73105

A Feeder System for a City

The Houston Independent Magnet Schools

Initiators	Houston Independent School District. Planning was done by the staff.
Funding	District taxes
Identification	*Elementary* General in nature, interest and aptitude as judged by teachers. *Junior High* Each of the four schools develops its own requirements. *Senior High, grades nine through twelve* Interviews with teachers and counselors, academic record, and observation of classroom behavior.
Goal	*Elementary and Junior High* To make students more aware of their community and local culture, both past and present, and to familiarize students with basic art techniques. *Senior High* To prepare students for various forms of higher education and careers. The program attempted to serve academic as well as artistic achievers.

Structure   Students at every level of the program have the following in common:

1. A full academic load in addition to daily art activity.
2. A choice between visual and performing arts in addition to many choices within the visual arts.
3. Bus transportation for field trips and in junior high school, to and from school.
4. Exposure to visiting artists, expanded audiovisual services, and art history.
5. The goal of integrating with different ethnic populations and receiving quality arts instruction.
6. The option of transferring from a general school to a magnet whenever they are ready.

Curriculum   Elementary art curriculum includes painting, ceramics, stitchery, drawing, and sculpture. These are expanded as the student moves to higher levels. The senior high school offers commercial art, photography, animation, color theory, fiber art, jewelrymaking, three years of art history, and graphics, in addition to the basic core of drawing, painting, sculpture, and printmaking. Curricula vary with the schools: one may stress the integrative aspects of the arts (Scroggins) and others may be more visual arts centered.

Evaluation   None described in report. Since teachers on one level are in close contact with those on the next, careful record keeping is a part of the plan.

Note   Houston Independent School District students are accepted from all private and public schools in Texas and also have pupils from sixteen other states and nine foreign countries. In all, there are 550 students. Ninety percent of its graduates go on to higher education in the arts and, to date, they have received over a million dollars in awards and scholarships.

Contact   Annette Wagispach Watson
Director of Art
Houston Independent School District
3830 Richmond Avenue
Houston, TX 77027

A State-Wide Program

A committee of concerned artists, craftspersons, and educators from both the *West Virginia Art Education Association* and the *West Virginia State Department of Education* conceived and carried out a plan for a two-week West Virginia Institute Art and Crafts for talented youth at Cedar Lakes, Ripley, West Virginia. They worked out a careful proposal, and by drawing from a number of sources (State Department of Education Title IX-State Talented and Gifted Funds, Bureau of Vocational Technical and Adult Education, West Virginia Arts and Humanities Commission and corporate and private donations) raised $47,873 to start the first state-centered program of its kind. (The six programs that already existed were non-selective and charged fees, however minimal.) The program eventually accomodated 110 students based on two from each county, or fourteen per region. All staff members were selected from a national rather than a local level and instructors were selected for their professional records as well as their abilities as teachers. An advisory committee of nineteen art educators in leading positions in the state was appointed and three arts-related administrators from the De partment of Education supervised the entire operation, although the institute operated under its own director. The Institute's goals were:

- the exploration and refining of an art or craft form
- the cultivation and appreciation of a variety of art or craft forms
- the formation of a value system for art or craft criticism and future growth
- the examination of creative problem-solving in an art or craft form
- the enrichment and acceleration of experience in art or crafts
- the creation of individual expression through art or craft forms
- the exploration of markets and the marketing of art and craft work
- the examination of careers and vocations in art or crafts

Each goal was further broken down into two objectives and the resultant outcome or learning behavior. As an example of how this was done, two of the goals are broken down here:

GOALS	OBJECTIVES	OUTCOMES
The creation of individual expression through art or craft forms.	The talented learner will employ skills to produce a unique work(s) in an art or craft form.	Given the opportunity to work in an art or craft form, the learner will exhibit unique individual expressions.
	The talented learner will interpret/explain a work he/she has created in an art or craft form.	Given an art or craft form, the learner will interpret and explain the relationship between the work and the concepts, ideas and attitudes it expresses.
The examination of careers and vocations in art or crafts.	The talented learner will analyze the educational and practical requirements for a career in art or crafts.	Given an art or craft occupation, the learner will discuss and identify the educational and practical requirements for a career in art or crafts.
	The talented learner will discuss and examine career opportunities in art or crafts.	Given an art or craft career, the learner will identify and compare career opportunities in a specific art or craft occupation.

Descriptive flyers and application materials were sent in February to each county superintendent, art supervisor, art teacher, and principal in the state. Also included were guidelines for identification of promising applicants as well as specific criteria to be used in evaluating applications: a personal statement, a teacher's recommendation, general student information, and a portfolio of work.

Student illustrations of a piece of imaginative writing.

General identification, which was expected to begin on the applicant's level, was based upon nine areas deemed significant: perception, performance, creativity, originality, flexibility, fluency, knowledge, skills, and commitment. Each of these was described in sufficient detail to assist in its recognition. Eight specific criteria for artwork were also described to give the student a clearer idea of what the judges would look for in their work:

- Originality of idea
- Originality of execution
- Understanding of design
- Evidence of depth of involvement in a specific area of interest
- Proficiency in breadth of involvement, i.e., experimentation with various media and varied approaches to one medium
- Technical proficiency
- Quantity as a variety of work
- Openness to new ideas

As for the curriculum, the Institute offers intensive courses in printmaking, painting, sculpture, photography, ceramics, textiles, weaving, jewelry, basketry, and woodworking. The number of craft courses represents local tradition and many courses offer three and four arts areas within them. The same introductory course is required of all students, but thereafter they select an art or craft major and a minor area such as mime, dance, or music. The formal critique replaced the conventional grading system and visiting artists are on hand to teach mini-sessions, lead discussion groups, and give demonstrations. Students are kept busy until 11 P.M. when lights are turned out. Evenings are filled with talent shows, media presentations, performances, drawing seminars, career presentations, films, and open discussion groups. The only cost to the student is transportation and pocket money.

National Programs for Gifted Secondary Students

Scholastic Art and Photography Awards   This is the oldest continuing program for the artistically gifted in existence (fifty-five years) and is the only one open from the seventh grade on. Scholastic has fifteen media classifications and makes distinctions between art and photography with special awards for sculpture and crafts. It begins with sixty regional exhibits over the country and ends with a national showing in New York City. Awards take the form of tuition scholarships, cash, and gold medals of recognition. This organization also has a number of filmstrips available for purchase that review the top-level winners.

If you want to study a unique record of changing interests of gifted students, compare the very first collection of winners with the latest one. The influence of current art trends will quickly become evident. An informal survey shows that in the late 1960s students were most interested in painting, abstract compositions, and crafts having utilitarian functions. Current interests emphasize drawing, illustration, airbrush, photographs and photo-realism, and crafts used in more personally expressive ways.

Advanced Placement   Any school in the country can participate in the Advanced Placement programs in Art History, General Studio Art, and Drawing, which are intended to provide college or art school levels of experience for high school students who intend to transfer credits earned in the program to an institution of higher education.

The AP program in Studio Art and Drawing requirements are divided into three parts: (A) original works; (B) a slide record and written commentary of an extended project of the student's choosing; and (C) a slide collection of works that deal with such problems as drawing skill, color, conceptual focus, space, and three-dimensional designs. There are no media limitations since students are encouraged to pursue their own interests, particularly in part B, which has produced projects in filmmaking, theater design, video art, murals, and other areas.

The structure of the AP programs as conducted throughout the country in public and private secondary schools reflect many patterns. The most used are as follows:

1. Informal tutorial relationship between one or two students and teacher

2. A selected group within a regular art class
3. A special class, meeting as a distinct group
4. A program created in conjunction with a museum
   (Example: Cleveland Museum of Art)

Arts Recognition and Talent Search (ARTS)

In 1979-80, the Educatonal Testing Service initiated the National Scholars in the Arts, a program for the recognition of graduating high school seniors who were highly accomplished in all of the arts.

In December '81, six hundred talented senior high school students submitted slides of their art work to a judging committee for the ARTS (Arts Recognition Talent Search) Program. Twenty semifinalists were selected from this group, and in January were flown to the University of Miami for ranking, the top four to receive the highest award of Presidential Scholars in the Arts. Music, drama, dance, and poetry were treated similarly. For the first time in the history of arts education in the United States, gifted students in the arts were gathered together in one location for a series of assessment tasks.

Each applicant was interviewed for 15 minutes by the committee of six judges. During this time students spoke informally about their work, artists they liked, future plans, etc. When not being interviewed, students worked independently on three assignments. In the three-dimensional design problem, they organized such materials as string, straw, balsa wood strips, and styrofoam balls. In the imaginative problem, students prepared an illustration for a passage of a literary work. Their still life pictures showed a section of a floor-to-ceiling still life. There was a wide range of interpretation. Finalists in each arts area were invited to Washington with their parents to receive both the Presidential Scholars Medallion and a cash award provided by the Geraldine Rockefeller Dodge Foundation. These awards were presented to the students by the President of the United States.

The ARTS program is but one function of the National Foundation for Advancement in the Arts (NFAA), a Miami-based organization, formed in 1981. The NFAA does fundraising for its programs and works with Educational Testing Service in the administration of the ARTS program.

The Foundation expects to develop a variety of other awards such as cash, scholarships, and workshop experiences, for which applicants will be eligible. The names of those meeting high standards of

A Zuni Indian semi-finalist for the ARTS Program demonstrated his ability to work in both traditional Indian and traditional realistic Western style. The judging of artwork which is created in any clearly defined ethnic mode presents problems that may not exist in judging the art work of the dominant culture.

This ceramic "people" pot and systems painting demonstrate the artist's curiosity about materials and techniques. They were created by Jonathan Cutler, one of the first winners of the National Scholars in the Arts program.

accomplishment will be further circulated to educational institutions to be considered for admission and scholarships. Semi-finalists and finalists will receive certificates of accomplishment.

The unique part of the ARTS program lies in the final selection of the four presidential winners. Each January, twenty semi-finalists are flown to Miami for several intensive days of interviews and studio assignments. Since the participants will have been selected from over 1400 applicants from the nation's high school art departments, it can be assumed that those who compete for the final award have a mastery of basic drawing skills, the use of color, and a particular medium. What may not be evident is the ability of the student to work independently, to think visually, and to make an original statement. The tasks devised for these students therefore attend to these issues as well as to conventional skills such as drawing, sensitivity to art, media, composition, color awareness, etc.

University-Supported Programs

One university-supported program worth noting is the "Solo Show" program offered by Clermont College of the University of Cincinnati to the students of the local school district. Students from the second to the twelfth grades may apply by submitting portfolios of work. Since quality of artwork alone is studied, anyone may apply without going through a screening process. Applicants and parents must complete a self-rating scale (see the appendix) and once selected, they are required to go through all the steps required to present an exhibition. This means designing their own programs and poster, sending out the invitations, and handling their own publicity. They must also organize their own "openings" and even handle their own refreshments. (Obviously, the older the child, the more is expected in the way of fulfilling these tasks.) Guidelines and suggestions are provided for the young exhibitors, and are quite detailed in the amount of information given. The college handles four such student shows a year.

"Super Saturday" offers students in elementary and junior high schools in the fourteen counties surrounding Purdue University in West Lafayette, Indiana an imaginative array of intensive short courses on Saturday mornings during the school year. This program

Students work on the sculpture
portion of the ARTS challenge.

is part of the Education Resource Institute at the university. Twenty-six courses are offered, four of them in the fine arts. Under the direction of staff members of the Department of Art Education, nine undergraduate and graduate students instruct the classes. This program is one of the very few that begins in the kindergarten and extends through the eighth grade.

The talents and expertise of the teachers determine the nature of the activities in the Purdue program. As an example, one group was involved in basic design activities, while another worked in ceramics. Other groups were offered a variety of arts and crafts activities including soft sculpture and puppetry. Recently, a large puppet stage was constructed and the children wrote and performed plays with the puppets they made. Older students have made animated films and studied drawing, painting, and printmaking in the university art studios. All groups tour an art museum each semester and have introductions to professional artists who describe their career.

The program is evaluated by the parents and children each semester and is a popular addition to private and public school programs for the gifted and talented in the Purdue area. The Purdue program is very similar to weekend programs provided by Pennsylvania State University and the Maryland Institute College of Art.

Appendix I
Sample Forms

These sample evaluation forms have been used in programs with successful records. The text of the Gifted and Talented Children's Education Program (84.080) has been included in its entirety for those who wish to seek funding from federal sources.

Gifted and Talented Children's Education Program (84.080)

Program Purpose

To meet the special educational needs of the nation's gifted and talented children, and enable these children to fulfill their potential both as individuals and as a resource to the nation.

Quick Check

Eligible Applicants	Type of Assistance
x SEA*	x Formula Grants
x LEA	x Project Grants
x IHE	x Contracts
x NPO	___ Cooperative
___ Other	Agreements

*SEAs may apply for only the State-Administered Grant Program, and Statewide Projects under the Discretionary Grant Program.

Essential Considerations

Allowable Activities: Funds may be used for the planning, development, operation, and improvement of programs to meet the needs of the gifted and talented children. Entry level internship allowances, graduate fellowship stipends, tuition and fees, inservice or leadership training, higher education fees and tuition for relevant courses, and substitute costs and release time are among the allowable costs.

Requirements and Restrictions: Any project involving the participation of gifted and talented children must use comprehensive and multiple identification and assessment methods. Any project involving an instructional component must provide differentiated or specialized services which specifically meet the special needs of such children and include curriculum content exceeding that which is regularly provided to the average student.

Under the State-Administered Grant Program, 90 percent of the funds received by the state must be competitively awarded to LEAs. The remaining 10 percent may be used for statewide planning, coordination, technical assistance, administration or inservice training. States must provide assistance to LEAs unable to compete for funding in proposal development, project planning and operation. Of the funds required to be passed through to LEAs, 50 percent must be awarded to projects that include a component for identifying and serving gifted and talented children from low-income families.

Funds may not be used for construction, remodeling or facility alteration, or stipends, transportation or meals for inservice participants.

Grant-Making Process

Administering Agency: U.S. Department of Education

Application Procedure: All applications are submitted to the Department of Education.

State-Administered Grant Program: - For a minimum formula grant allotment of $50,000 the state must submit general assurances and a plan for making competitive subgrants meeting the above requirements. To receive additional funds the state must include a special section in its application which responds to the evaluation criteria for annual competitive state grants.

Discretionary Grant Program - Three types of projects will be considered for support based upon announced annual priorities.
Statewide Projects may be designed for one or more of the following activities: 1. develop a comprehensive statewide approach, 2. involve parent and other organizations in gifted and talented education, 3. develop innovative strategies, 4. provide technical assistance to public and private schools, 5. conduct surveys of needs and programs, 6. provide a state coordinator for local programs, and 7. develop and implement inservice training.
Educational Service or Model Projects must: 1. provide for the operation, expansion or improvement of gifted and talented education, 2. the use of innovative or model approaches, and as appropriate, 3. have capability for cost effectiveness and replicability, 4. provide related inservice training, 5. involve non-school individuals and organizations, 6. be based on an existing high quality project, 7. focus on special populations, and 8. focus on a particular category of service.
Professional Development Projects shall provide: 1. a variety of short-term courses and instruction, 2. seminars and other opportunities for educators to interact with leaders in other fields, 3. internships and other practical training experiences, 4. inservice training, 5. issue related workshops and conferences with broad-based participation, and 6. development of specialized training materials.

Selection Criteria: State-Administered Grant Program - Competitive State Grants are reviewed based upon the selection criteria weighted as follows: 1. Comprehensive approach to identifying and meeting needs under the competitive subgrant process (25 points), 2. Planning which involves broad participation in developing subgrant award procedures (15 points), 3. Technical Assistance quality in assisting LEAs unable to compete for subgrants (20 points), 4. Administration reflected in the quality of

the subgrant award process (15 points), 5. Disadvantaged service plan
(10 points), and 6. Coordination and monitoring of LEA activities and
dissemination of results (15 points).

Discretionary Grant Program applications are reviewed as follows:
 Statewide Projects are reviewed based upon the EDGAR criteria weighted
 on a 100 point scale:
 1. Plan of Operation (35 points),
 2. Quality of Key Personnel (25 points),
 3. Budget and Cost Effectiveness (15 points),
 4. Evaluation Plan (15 points), and
 5. Adequacy of Resources (10 points).

All Other Applications are reviewed on a 100 point scale based upon
EDGAR Criteria (30 points) –
 1. Plan of Operation (10 points),
 2. Quality of Key Personnel (7 points),
 3. Budget and Cost Effectiveness (5 points), and
 4. Adequacy of Resources (3 points).

Program Criteria (70 points)
 1. Level and Quality of Program (25 points) – comprehensive nature
     of the specialized services, or skills of the participating
     personnel,
 2. Selection of Participants (15 points) – procedures for identifica-
     tion and selection,
 3. Specially Trained Personnel, Mentors or Advisors (15 points) –
     qualifications and use of those who will direct or assist
     participants,
 4. Replication (5 points),
 5. Dissemination (5 points), and
 6. Needs Assessment (5 points).

Closing Date: FY81 deadlines are February 3, 1981 for State Administered
 Minimum Grants (new and continuation) and new State Grants, and February 17,
 1981 for Professional Development Grants (new and continuation), Model.
 Projects (new) and Statewide Activities (new).

Award Information

Range of Awards: $15,000 to $400,000

Average Award: $62,000

Competition: Statewide Projects – 24 applications and 11 awards; Educational Service or
 Model Projects – 128 applications and 4
 awards; and Professional Development Projects
 – 52 applications and 11 awards.

Funding Levels
 FY81 Appropriation: n/a
 FY81 Budget Request: $6.28M
 FY80 Appropriation: $6.28M

Project Duration:
 State-Administered Grant
 Program
 Formula Grants – three yrs.
 Competitive Grants-one yr.
 Discretionary Grants-Up to
                      five yrs.

Citations

<u>Legislative Authority</u>: Title IX, Part A of the Elementary and Secondary
                              Education Act, as amended by Public Law 95-561.

<u>Regulations</u>: 45 CFR 195, published in the <u>Federal Register</u>, Vol. 45,
               No. 66, on April 3, 1980.

Information Contacts

<u>Headquarters Office</u>: Dr. Harold Lyon, Jr., Director
                        Gifted and Talented Children's Education Program
                        U.S. Department of Education
                        400 Maryland Ave., SW
                        Room 2837 - Donohoe
                        Washington, DC 20202
                        Phone: 202-245-2482

Personal Characteristics Appraisal

PERSONAL CHARACTERISTICS APPRAISAL

KENMORE-TOWN OF TONAWANDA UNION FREE SCHOOL DISTRICT

Name_____School_____Grade_____

Date_____Person completing form_____

LEARNING STRENGTHS

1. Thinks logically and/or critically.
2. Retains for a long period and has quick recall of factual information.
3. Shows insight; is observant.
4. Has a large storehouse of information.
5. Transfers learning easily from one subject area to another.
6. Functions at higher cognitive levels with little frustration.
7. Masters basic skills easily and quickly.
8. Is intuitive; understands with little or no apparent effort.
9. Enjoys learning; is curious.
10. Has advanced oral, written, and/or reading vocabulary.

SOCIAL-EMOTIONAL STRENGTHS

11. Adapts readily to new situations; is flexible in thought and action.
12. Tends to show more than usual interest in ethical/philosophical issues.
13. Self-confident, mature.
14. Sociable; gregarious.
15. Has a sense of humor; enjoys contradictions/paradoxes.
16. Is cooperative.
17. Relates well with peers and adults who have similar interests.
18. Has high personal standards; takes pride in self/work.
19. Directive; shows leadership.
20. Is responsible; reliable.

GENERAL WORK-STUDY STRENGTHS

21. Is attentive.
22. Is highly motivated, seeks new tasks/activities.
23. Is resourceful.
24. Is spontaneous; can improvise.
25. Has high tolerance for ambiguity.
26. Has self-discipline.
27. Seeks to improve areas of need.
28. Assignments are done well, and on time.
29. Is well organized; plans and uses time to advantage.
30. Is a good problem solver.

PRODUCTION STRENGTHS

(In this area, please consider only those activities conducted within the classroom or school setting.)

31. Is task committed; persevering.
32. Highly productive; accomplishes goals.
33. Is a problem "finder"; inquires about many/varied topics.
34. Generates more than one idea for/or solution to a problem.
35. Is original in thought and expression.
36. Meets deadlines with ease; needs little or no reminding.
37. Is able to set goals for self in relation to production.
38. Uses imaginative methods.
39. Constructs models, charts, graphs or visual materials to supplement work.
40. Creates stories, books, or writes poetry.

1. Do you recommend this child for a G/T program? (circle one)

    Without Reservation   With Reservation   No

    Reasons for choice:_____

2. List any special interest areas child has_____

3. List any areas recommended for acceleration:_____

4. If you are aware of any honors, awards, etc. child has received for outstanding work, please list them:_____

5. Check any of the following elements of creative thinking in which child shows unusual ability:
    _____ fluency (produces many ideas)
    _____ Flexibility (classifies ideas into categories, sees relationships between categories)
    _____ elaboration (embellishes upon ideas, adds details)
    _____ originality (has unique ideas)

    In what area(s) does child exhibit creative behavior? Give examples if possible:
    _____

6. List any other descriptors applicable to this child:_____
    _____

7. Many factors affect a child's performance in a program. If you are aware of any other information you feel is pertinent in the selection process, please indicate below:_____

Interview Form: Attitudinal Component for Candidates in Visual Arts Program

INTERVIEW FORM: ATTITUDINAL COMPONENT FOR CANDIDATES IN VISUAL ARTS PROGRAM

STATE OF GEORGIA
DEPARTMENT OF EDUCATION
STATE OFFICE BUILDING
ATLANTA, GEORGIA 30334

_____
FINAL RATING

NAME_____

SIGNATURE OF INTERVIEWERS_____

Rate the nominee with regard to the five statements listed below, as evidenced by your interview of the nominee. Rate each statement on a scale of 1 to 5 as referenced below. You must write evidences to support your rating in each category. The sum of the numerical ratings for each statement is the nominee's total interview score. Place this in the space provided. (1) strongly disagree, (2) disagree, (3) undecided, (4) agree, (5) strongly agree.

1.   The nominee exhibits the personal maturity necessary for a GHP participant.

   1 2 3 4 5 Evidences to support rating:_____

2.   The nominee exhibits a genuine desire to participate in GHP.

   1 2 3 4 5 Evidences to support rating:_____

3.   The student exhibits a positive attitude toward art and artists.

   1 2 3 4 5 Evidences to support rating:_____

4.   The student exhibits evidence of a high level of interest, involvement and participation in school and community art activities.

   1 2 3 4 5 Evidences to support rating:_____

5.   The student exhibits an open-mindedness toward artistic experimentation (flexibility, curiosity).

   1 2 3 4 5 Evidences to support rating:_____

6.   My general, overall impression of this nominee as a potential GHP participant was favorable.

   1 2 3 4 5 Evidences to support rating other than those in items 1 through 4:

   _____

READ BY INTERVIEWER:

   I.   Teacher Recommendations

  II.   Student Comments

 III.   Grades and Courses

Assessment of Student Prior to Attending a Program

ASSESSMENT OF STUDENT PRIOR TO ATTENDING A PROGRAM

AMERICAN MOSAIC CLASS TEST

1. Have you ever read or looked at an art book or art magazine in a store, school or the Public Library?_____

2. Do you remember one that you enjoyed the most?_____

3. Have you been to any of the following places: The Detroit Art Institute, the Detroit Historical Museum, the Children's Museum, Your Heritage House, the Cranbrook Art Gallery, Greenfield Village, the University of Michigan Art Museum or the Kelsey Museum in Ann Arbor?_____If so, which_____

4. Do you have a favorite museum, artist or art era from the past that you remember from your visit?_____

5. Have you ever drawn, painted or made a statue or craftwork at home or in school that was your own idea?_____ If so, briefly describe the work.

6. Can you describe which of the above activities interested you the most, and tell us why?_____

7. Can you point out three made items and three natural items in daily life which are artful objects?_____

MATCH THE FOLLOWING NUMBER WITH THE CORRECT LETTER:

_____ 1. King Tut   A. An African Kingdom famous for its bronze statues.

_____ 2. Parthenon   B. A woven picture.

_____ 3. Mona Lisa   C. An outdoor architectural space.

_____ 4. Benin   D. A Greek Temple.

_____ 5. Picasso   E. A famous Detroit Architect.

_____ 6. The Thinker   F. A famous portrait by Leonardo DaVinci.

_____ 7. Mural   G. A wall picture.

_____ 8. Plaza   H. A famous statue by Rodin, in front of the Art Institute.

_____ 9. Yamasaki   I. A famous Egyptian Pharaoh noted for his beautiful tomb objects.

_____10. Tapestry   J. A famous 20th Century artist.

A Visual Assessment

1A ☐　Conflict　1B ☐　　　2A ☐　Calm　2B ☐

3A ☐　Depth　3B ☐　　　4A ☐　Distance　4B ☐

 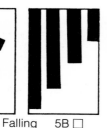  

5A ☐　Falling　5B ☐　　　6A ☐　Rhythm　6B ☐

   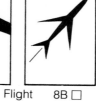   

7A ☐　Order　7B ☐　　　8A ☐　Flight　8B ☐

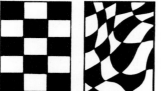  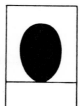

9A ☐　Movement　9B ☐　　　10A ☐　Stability　10B ☐

1　Your sense of design

Here are ten pairs of designs. Study each pair carefully. Place a check mark under the design which you feel *better* illustrates the meaning of the word. Check only one design in each pair. When finished, you should have checked ten pictures.

Grade_____

BOARD OF EDUCATION OF FREDERICK COUNTY

115 East Church Street
FREDERICK, MARYLAND 21701

Instruction

Telephone
694-1341

October, 1979

Dear

    It is my pleasure to inform you that _____
has been accepted in the Title IV Gifted and Talented Program for Frederick
County this year. We have only selected a limited number of students and
look forward to a very challenging program. Mr. Joseph Osmann, Instructor
at Governor Thomas Johnson High School, will be in charge. A copy of the
program, dates and events is enclosed. Please keep this posted and be a-
ware of the content.

    Your major responsibility will be seeing that _____
has safe transportation to and from each evening session. The project will
pay for all instructors, materials and field trips, which gives your child
at least a $300.00 scholarship.

    Again, I extend my sincere congratulations to _____
for being nominated by the Art Instructor and being selected in our 1979-80
program.

    Since the first class starts soon (October 30), I am asking you to
confirm your status by filling out the enclosed permission form and mailing
it to my office by October 29th. You may wish to call my office at 694-1341
and confirm the acceptance or refusal. Your cooperation is greatly appreciated.

            Sincerely,

            Carroll H. Kehne, Jr.
            Art Education Curriculum Specialist

- -

PERMISSION SLIP

_____ has my permission to participate in the

CONTINUING ART PROGRAM as part of the Gifted and Talented Project in Frederick
County.

              _____
                   Parent/Guardian

PLEASE RETURN TO CARROLL KEHNE.

Criteria for Awarding Student Honors

CRITERIA FOR AWARDING STUDENT HONORS

STATE OF GEORGIA
DEPARTMENT OF EDUCATION
STATE OFFICE BUILDING
ATLANTA, GA 30334

CRITERIA FOR SELECTION OF VISUAL ARTS FINALIST
GOVERNOR'S HONORS PROGRAM

The following Visual Arts criteria will be used by interview teams in selecting finalists for the Governor's Honors Program. Local coordinators may wish to use these criteria in making local nominations. Program nominees must be in the tenth or eleventh grade.

FINE ARTS: VISUAL ARTS

GENERAL CRITERIA   EVIDENCE

1. The student exhibits initiative and   Interviews student applica-
    commitment toward learning and the   tion. Teacher recommenda-
    desire to study the visual arts.   tion.

2. The student must evidence high achieve-   Interview. Teacher recom-
    ment in the visual arts identified by: mendation. Student appli-
    a) imaginative and creative works of   cation.
       art produced by the student

    b) classroom performance (art know-
       ledge and attitude)

3. The student demonstrates the ability to   Interview. Student appli-
    work independently in both the regularly   cation. Teacher recommen-
    assigned work and in self-motivated study.   dation.

4. The student is willing and able to pursue   Interview. Teacher recom-
    in-depth study over an extended period of   mendation. Student appli-
    time.   cation.

5. The student exhibits original thinking   Interview. Teacher recom-
    in solving problems and in learning new   mendation. Student appli-
    ideas.   cation.

6. The student exhibits the background and   Interview. Teacher recom-
    ability to critically respond to works   mendation. Student appli-
    of art.   cation.

Presentation

Visual art nominees will be interviewed by a selected team of art educators. At
the time of the interview, the student should bring the following:

1. <u>Original art works</u> selected by the student (no number limitations) (Two-
    dimensional works should be matted or presented in a portfolio).

2. Photographs of the student's art work neatly mounted on sturdy poster board
    type paper (approximately 22" X 28"). A printed or typed brief description
    of the work should be under each photograph listing (a) size; (b) media and
    (c) nature of class assignment, if assigned by a teacher. A photograph of
    the student should be mounted in the upper left-hand corner with the student's
    name, school address, age and grade level under the photograph.

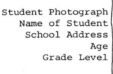 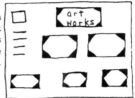

                Student Photograph
                Name of Student
                School Address
                Age
                Grade Level

Procedures for Interview Day

     Art students will report to the designated interview center at the scheduled
time (8:00 am or 1:00 pm as scheduled by the GHP office) for the art registration.
Students will exhibit work in an assigned area and will engage in discussions with
a team of interviewers at the specified time for his/her individual interview. Easels,
tables, and other display supplies are not provided at the interview center.

     Upon completion of the interview, the students will remove their art works from
the display area leaving the mounted photographs in the possession of the interview team.

     The photographs will be returned after June 1 provided the photographs can
be easily removed from their surface and a self-addressed, stamped envelope or
mailing folder is presented to the interviewers. Photo tabs are suggested for
providing easy removal of student photographs.

Specific Categories To Be Measured

        A. Interview Form: Art knowledge and skills component   60 points

        B. Interview Form: Attitudinal Component   30 points

        C. Application Information & Other Evidences   10 points

                                                          Total 100 points possible

Student Reaction Form

STUDENT REACTION FORM

PROJECT ART BAND - DE CORDOVA MUSEUM

STUDENT REACTION SURVEY

Name_____Grade_____

School_____

For each of the following questions, choose the correct response or the response that best describes your feelings.

1. From the list below, place a check next to those statements that best describe your experiences with your artist.

   _____ I helped the artist do his/her work.

   _____ I received instruction from the artist as if it were a private art class.

   _____ I did my own work and the artist did his/her own work.

   _____ Other, please explain?

   _____

   _____

2. Which **artist** are you working with this year?

   _____

For questions 3 through 11 use the following scale of responses: (1) strongly disagree, (2) disagree, (3) slightly agree, (4) agree, (5) strongly agree.

3. I would like to be an artist. 1 2 3 4 5

4. I enjoy being in a class with other students who really like art. 1 2 3 4 5

5. I know a great deal about what is involved in the work of our artist. 1 2 3 4 5

6. I am learning many new skills and techniques from my artist. 1 2 3 4 5

7. Art-Band class is much more advanced and challenging than other art classes. 1 2 3 4 5

8. Most art is enjoyable. 1 2 3 4 5

9. I think we should spend more time on art in my school. 1 2 3 4 5

10. I look forward to visiting the Boston Museum of Fine Arts. 1 2 3 4 5

11. I don't mind making up work that I missed in order to take art lessons in my school. 1 2 3 4 5

12. Describe some of the differences between the Art-Band class and other art classes.

_____

_____

_____

_____

13. When I go to an art museum, I:

_____ a.) really enjoy visiting it.

_____ b.) find it boring.

_____ c.) am usually forced to go by my teacher or parents.

_____ d.) feel like kids are not welcome in museums.

14. Architecture is:

_____ a.) the study of the feet

_____ b.) an historical period

_____ c.) a form of dance

_____ d.) the study of classical music

_____ e.) the style and design of buildings

15. Texture is the word for:

_____ a.) shapes

_____ b.) shades

_____ c.) tints

_____ d.) surfaces

A Museum Program Evaluation

WASHINGTON TOWNSHIP ART ENRICHMENT PILOT

SCULPTURE: SPACE AND TIME ENOUGH:

We at the Indianapolis Museum of Art, staff and docents, have appreciated our
time together with you and hope that you have enjoyed your experiences with the
Museum and its works of art! We hope that you've come to know and understand
sculpture as a very special art form and as a member of the family of arts.

So that we may best explore sculpture with visitors in the future, we would like
you to answer the few short questions below about the four experiences which you
have shared with us.

DAY ONE - "WHAT IS SCULPTURE?" (Circle your favorite part of the day)

    1. Introduction and Slide Show
    2. Gallery walk
    3. Talk with the artist, Mike Helbing
    4. Making your drawing!

What was your least favorite activity (circle) 1   2   3   4

Did you learn any new terms? (circle)   Yes   No

Can you list, any?_____

_____

What would you change about the day?_____

_____

What is sculpture to you?_____

_____

DAY TWO - "HOW IS SCULPTURE MADE?" What part did you enjoy the most? (Please circle)

    1. Megan O'Hara - ceramics
    2. Karl Chenowith - wood
    3. Mike Helbing - construction
    4. Roger White - modeling and casting
    5. All

What new things did you learn (terms, ideas, ways to do sculpture)?_____

_____

_____

What do you remember most?_____

_____

_____

-2-

Evaluation Form

DAY THREE - "WHY SCULPTURE?"

What activity did you enjoy most? (Please circle)

    1. Introduction and slide presentation
    2. Gallery walk
    3. Wrap sesson

What was your least favorite activity? (circle)   1   2   3

Why do you think sculpture was made?_____

_____

_____

What do you remember most?_____

_____

What would you change about the day?_____

_____

_____

DAY IV - "SCULPTURE NOW ON..."

What part of the day did you enjoy most? (Please circle)

    1. Introduction and slide presentation
    2. Sculpture walk
    3. Body sculptures
    4. Discussion and ending

What did you enjoy least? (circle)   1   2   3   4

Why do you think we make sculpture today?_____

_____

_____

What would you change about the day?_____

_____

Would you visit the Museum again on your own (circle)   Yes   No

Would you bring your family/friends? (circle)   Yes   No

Appendix II
Organizations

Advanced Placement Program in Studio Art, Drawing and Art History
Educational Testing Service
Princeton, New Jersey 08541

American Association for Gifted Children (AAGC)
15 Gramercy Park
New York, New York 10003
Contact: Marjorie Craig, vice-president and executive director,
        Gail Robinson, staff assistant, (212) 473-4266

Council for Exceptional Children/ERIC Clearinghouse on Handicapped
and Gifted Children (CEC/ERIC)
1920 Association Drive
Reston, Virginia 22091
Contact: Lynn Smarte, information specialist, (800) 336-3728,
        (703) 620-3660

Creative Education Foundation
State University College at Buffalo
218 Chase Hall
1300 Elmwood Avenue
Buffalo, New York 14222
Contact: Donald Treffinger, (716) 878-6221

National Association for Gifted Children
217 Gregory Drive
Hot Springs, Arkansas 71901

National Foundation for the Advancement of the Arts
100 North Biscayne Boulevard, Suite 2302
Miami, Florida 33132

National State Leadership Training Institute on the Gifted and the Talented
316 West Second Street, Suite PH-C
Los Angeles, California 90012
Contact: Irving Sato, director, (213) 489-7470

Office of Gifted and Talented
U.S. Office of Education (USOE)
Washington, D.C. 20202
Contact: Dorothy Sisk, (202) 245-2482

Office of Talented Identification and Development (OTID)
Johns Hopkins University
Baltimore, Maryland 21218
Contact: William George, director, (301) 338-7087

Bibliography

The following books and articles on giftedness were written from the perspective of art educators and psychologists.

Eisner, Elliot W. *Educating Artistic Vision.* New York: Macmillan Co., 1972

Gardner, Howard. *Artful Scribbles: The Significance of Children's Drawings.* New York: Basic Books, Inc., 1980.

Gaitskell, Charles D.; Hurwitz, Al; and Day, Michael. *Children and Their Art: Methods for the Elementary School.* 4th rev. ed. New York: Harcourt Brace and Jovanovich, Inc., 1982.

Getzels, Jacob W., and Csikszentmihalyi, Mihaly. *Creative Vision: A Longitudinal Study of Problem Finding in Art.* New York: John Wiley and Sons, Inc., 1976.

Lark-Horovitz, B.; Lewis, H.; and Luca, M. *Understanding Children's Art for Better Teaching.* 2d ed. Columbus, Ohio: Charles E. Merrill Publishing Co., 1973.

Mendelowitz, David. *Children are Artists: An Introduction to Children's Art for Teachers and Parents.* 2d rev. ed. Stanford, California: Stanford University Press, 1963.

Munro, T.; Lark-Horovitz, B.; and Barnhart, E.N. *Children's Art Abilities, Studies of the Cleveland Museum of Art.* Cleveland, Ohio: Cleveland Museum of Art, 1942.

NAEA National Career Education Committee, Four Monographs. Project Director, Charles M. Dorn. Reston, Virginia: National Art Education Association, 1980.

Passow, A.H. *The Gifted and the Talented: Their Education and Development.* 78th yearbook of the National Society for the Study of Education, Part I. Chicago, Illinois: The University of Chicago Press, 1979. See J. Getzell's "From Art Student to Fine Artist."

Renzulli, Joseph S. "Talent Potential in Minority Group Children." Special report for the Connecticut Department of Education. Hartford, Connecticut.

Renzulli, Joseph S. "What Makes Giftedness: Reexamining a Definition." *Phi Delta Kappan* 60, no. 3 (November 1978): 180-184.

Stake, Robert E., ed. *Evaluating the Arts.* Columbus, Ohio: Charles E. Merrill Publishing Co., 1975.

Torrance, E. Paul. *Guiding Creative Talent.* Melbourne, Florida: Robert E. Krieger Publishing Co., Inc., 1976.

U.S. Department of Education. *Education of the Gifted and Talented.* Report to Congress. Washington, D.C.: Government Printing Office, 1972.

Periodicals

Gifted Child Quarterly, 8980 Springvalley Drive, Cincinnati, Ohio 45236.
Journal for the Education of the Gifted, 1920 Association Drive, Reston, Virginia 22091.
School Arts Magazine, 50 Portland St., Worcester, Massachusetts 01608.

Measuring ability

The following tests are designed to identify gifted and talented students. It is recommended that the reader examine a sample copy of each to determine if the nature of the test is suitable for the type of student to be evaluated.

Art Vocabulary. Grades 6-12; 1969; R.H. Silverman, R. Hoepfner, and M. Hendricks. (Monitor, P.O. Box 2337, Hollywood, California 90028.)
Eisner Art Information and Attitude Test. Elementary and secondary; Dr. Elliot W. Eisner, Professor of Education and Art. (Contact author: College of Education, Stanford University, Stanford, California 94305.)
Flanagan Aptitude Classification Test, No. 18. Grades 9-12. Measures creativity or inventiveness,. (Science Research Associates Inc., 155 N. Wacker Dr., Chicago, Illinois 60606.)
The Meier Art Tests. Grades 7-16 and adults, 9-16 and adults; 1929-1963; Norman Charles Meier. Two tests: "The Meier Art Tests: 1 Art Judgment," Grades 7-16 and adults, and "The Meier Art Tests: 2: Aesthetic Perception," Grades 9-16 and adults. (Bureau of Educational Research and Service. Univeristy of Iowa, Iowa City, Iowa 52242.)
Project Talent Creativity Test. Grades 9-12. Stresses inventiveness. (Science Research Associates, Inc., 155 N. Wacker Dr., Chicago, Illinois 60606.)
Torrance Tests of Creative Thinking, Research Edition. Kindergarten through graduate school; 1966; E. Paul Torrance. "Figural Test: Thinking Creatively with Pictures." (Personnel Press, Education Center, P.O. Box 2649, Columbus, Ohio 43216.)
The Rutgers Drawing Test (RTD). Ages 4-6, 6-9; Anne Spiesman Starr. (Contact author: 126 Montgomery St., Highland Park, New Jersey 08904)

For a more complete listing of tests, see:
Buros, Oscar K. *Tests in Print—One*. Lincoln, Nebraska: University of Nebraska Press, 1961, and Buros, Oscar K. *Tests in Print—Two*. Lincoln, Nebraska: University of Nebraska Press, 1974.

Articles

Alexander, Robin, "An Historical Perspective on the Gifted and Talented and Art," *Studies in Art Education*, 1981.

Kay, Sandra, "The Gifted and the Arts: A Prismatic View," *School Arts*, February, 1982.

Lucia, Mark C. and Allen, Bonnie, "Teaching Gifted Children Art in Grades 4 through 6," Sacramento: Eric Document Reproduction Service, ED088254, 1973.

Saunders, Robert, "Screening and Identifying the Talented in Art," *Roper Review*, 1982.

General

Office of the Gifted and Talented—Public Law 93–380, Section 404—Special Projects, Washington D.C., 1979.

Doctoral Dissertation

Dunard, Juliette E.L., "Art and the Gifted Child, A Guide to Program Planning, A Study to Develop and to Determine the Effectiveness of the Multi-faceted Procedure for the Identification of Artistically Gifted and Creative Elementary School Students." George Washington University, School of Education and Human Development, 1982.

Index

Advanced placement, 23, 32, 35, 42, 68, 117
American Association of Architects, 37
American Crafts Council, 37
Anecdotal records, 87
Art
  centered tasks, 57
  Director's Club, 37
  history, in curriculum, 64
  representational, 77
Art Education, Journal of the NAEA, 39
Art Institute of Chicago, 18
Artists' Equity, 37
Arts and Activities, 93
Arts Recognition Talent Search, 23, 32, 49, 50, 118
Assessment, composite, 84
Awards
  National Scholastic, 23, 32
  photography, 117
  Scholastic Art, 117

Bacon, Francis, 100
Baker, David, 110
Bell, Winifred, 102
Bennett, Norma, 106
Bigelow Junior High School, 96
Bronzino, Agnolo, 63

California Institute of the Arts, 38
Cane, Florence, 55
Chinian, Matthew, 73
Cleveland Museum of Art, 6
Color sensitivity, 57
Comic strips, 24
Compositional control, 24
Concentration, 20
Consortium, 108
Cornell, Joseph, 67
Counseling Centre for Gifted Children of New York University, 55
Curriculum, 61-79
Cutler, Jonathan, 119

Daumier, Honoré, 29
David, Jacques-Louis, 74
da Vinci, Leonardo, 6, 52, 67
Dawes School, 102
Day, Michael, 27
DeCordova Museum, 108, 110, 134

Delacroix, Ferdinand, 74
Design
  awareness of, 72
  Program, General Motors, 38
Disney, Walt, 38

Educational Testing Service, 118
Education Resource Institute, 121
Ernst, Max, 78
Evaluations. *See* Tests and evaluations
Examinations
  centrally conducted, 59
  portfolio, 86
"Exemplar approach," 29
Exhibitions, 65

Fluency, 16, 22, 72
Francesco, Piero della, 29
Frates, Mary Y., 112
Funding
  corporate, 38
  school-level, 34

Gaitskell, Charles, D., 27
Gardner, Howard, 13, 14, 17, 22
Georgia
  criteria for honors selection in, 131
  interview form, Department of Education, 128
Geraldine Rockefeller Dodge Foundation, 118
Getzell, 27
Gifted and Talented
  children, attention for, pro and con, 8
  Children's Act of 1978, 36
  Children's Education Program, 37
  identification of. *See* identification
Gifted Child Quarterly, 93
Giftedness, assessment of, 16
Goals, 62-64
Goodenough-Harris. *See* Tests, "Draw a Man"
Goodman, Marilyn, 99
Gorki, Arshile, 78
Governor's Honors Program, 50, 131
Grant-making process, 123
Group critique, 64

Horowitz, Betty Lark, 7
Houston, P.D., 39

Identification of the gifted
   art-centered tasks, 57
   interview, 49
   methods, 43-59
   New York State Guidlines for, 103
   nonselective system, 44
   peer, 47
   self-evaluation, 51
   self-selective system, 44
   tests, 45
Improvisation, 27
Indianapolis Museum of Art, 104
Ingres, Jean Auguste Dominique, 68
International Baccalaureate Secondary
   Diploma, 23

Journal of Aesthetic Education, 29

Kehne, Carol, 100, 130
Kenmore Personal Characteristics
   Appraisal Instrument, 55
Kerr Foundation, 111
Kulpinsky, Barbara, 102
Kwasnick, Sue, 97

Lyon, Dr. Harold, Jr., 121

Matisse, Henri, 68, 100
Memory, 22, 26, 57, 72
Meyler, Joanna, 97
Michelangelo, 63
Milwaukee Art Center, 106
Minnesota Education Association, 47
Mondrian, Piet, 72
Motherwell, Robert, 78
Mozart, Amadeus, 20
Munro, Thomas, 7
Mythology, 41

Nadia, 20, 21
National Art Assessment of Educational
   Progress: art objectives, 53
National Art Education Association, 38
National Art Honors Society, 34
National Foundation for Advancement
   in the Arts, 118
New York Board of Education, 6
New York State, 15, 36, 37, 45

Oklahoma State Arts Council, 111

Oklahoma Summer Arts Institute, 111
Onada, Masami, 13

Pennsylvania State University, 51
Personal characteristics appraisal, 126
Phillips Petroleum Corporation, 38, 111
Picasso, Pablo, 68, 74
Pollack, Jackson, 78
Poussin, 74
Presidential Scholars in the Arts, 118
Project Art Band, 108, 134

Quartz Mountain School, 38

Renzulli, Joseph, 17
Rubens, Peter Paul, 29

Scales.   *See* Tests and evaluations
Scholastic ability, 45
Scholder, Fritz, 111
School Arts, 93
Schools without walls, 81
Self-directedness, 20
Selfe, Lorna, 27
Self-evaluation, 51
Self-portrait, 70
Sensitivity
   critical, 28
   to art media, 26
Shakespeare, William, 103
Smith, Ralph, 29
"Solo Show," 120
Spatial awareness, 19
Spitz, Ellen Handler, 104
State Arts Council of Oklahoma, 38
Student reaction form, 134, 135
"Super Saturday," 120

Tallchief, Marcia, 111
Tests and evaluations
   American Mosaics Class, 129
   "Draw a Man," Goodenough-Harris,
      23
   for creative thinking, 45
   form, 136– 37
   formative, 84
   Iowa, of Basic Skills, 45
   Iowa Verbal and Mathematical Abili-
      ties, 103
   Metropolitan Achievement, 45

model, 90
   National Assessment of Art, 110
   objective, 88
   Piers-Harris Self-Concept, 110
   preordinate, 84
   Renzuli-Hartmen, 104
   responsive, 84
   results, using, 59
   Stanford-Binet I.Q., 45
   summative, 84
   Torrance, of Creative Thinking, 46,
      108
Texture, 69
Torrance, Paul, 45

U.S. Department of Education, 15–17

Van Gogh, Vincent, 91, 108
Verisimilitude, 23

Walsh, Jeanne, 102
Watson, Annette, 113
West Virginia Art Education Associa-
   tion, 114
West Virginia State Department of
   Education, 114
White, Caroline, 107
Williams Cognitive Affective Inter-
   action Model, 48
Williams, Frank, 48
Wilson, Brent, 54
Wilson Cognitive Instrument, 51

Zuni, 119

Acknowledgements

I would like to thank the following persons who have made a contribution to this book: Francene Meredith and the staffs of Educational Testing Service and the National Foundation for the Advancement of the Arts gave assistance in processing examples of student work in the Advanced Placement Program in Drawing and the Arts Recognition Talent Search program.

Chris Small, David Fitzgerald, Bob Arruda, Vicki Maggio, and Steve Kucharski supplied photographic services without which the book would have been impossible to produce. Teachers such as Carolyn White, Mimi Jenkinson, Willard Robinson, Ramond Lavin, Mary Perkins, Davida Movitz, George Roberts, Bob Andrews, and Steven Hughes were of inestimable help in supplying both visual and written material, as were administrators David Baker, Joe Moody, Pat Zeitoun, Ellen Handler Spitz, Jacqueline Hinchey, Pat Moreno and Carrol Kehne.

Assistance from abroad came from many teachers and administrators. I have only the warmest memories of the following hosts and colleagues: Eddie Price, Jane Whinnie and Ray Thorburn, Andrea Karpati and Magda Koltai, Valentina Hadushina, Jack Meyer, and Jeffrey Verne. The staff of the International Baccalaureate Program also provided assistance.

Brent and Marjorie Wilson provided useful critical comments in the early stages of writing. Gilbert Clark, Richard Doornick, and Richard Freeland were particularly thorough in their critiques of the later stages of writing.

I would like to recognize the National Art Education Association for supporting me in my effort to initiate the first mini-conference on the subject of giftedness in art at the 1980 NAEA convention.